Jinx at the Greenbrier

Jinx at the Greenbrier

Deanna Edens

Acknowledgments

Special thanks to Geneva Lacy, Nancy Holloway, Barbara L. Jones, Pam Tindell, David Robert Edens Jr., and Ella Bokey for providing editing advice.
For professional, friendly and reasonably priced editing services, contact Susan Pilski at spilski@rocketmail.com

Cover photograph of the Greenbrier in 1916
https://commons.wikimedia.org/wiki/File%3AGreenbrier_Hotel_1916_cph.3b19148.jpg

Photo of Jinx by iuliia29photo at Deposit Photos

Some of the anecdotal illustrations in this book are true to life and are included with the permission of the persons involved. Additionally, all portrayals of people living or dead are dramatic renditions of actual historical events. This book is a work of fiction.

Other Books by Deanna Edens

The Convenience of Crafting Maple Fudge
Welcome to Bluewater Bay
Christmas Comes to Bluewater Bay
Mystery in Bluewater Bay
Love Blooms in Bluewater Bay
The Adventures of the Bluewater Bay Sequinettes:
The Complete Bluewater Bay Series
Angels of the Appalachians
Molly's Memoir
Erma's Attic: Angels of the Appalachians Book Two
Rosa's Castle

"If history were told in the form of stories,
it would never be forgotten."
— *Rudyard Kipling*

Jinx at the Greenbrier

A Note from the Author

I HAVE ALWAYS enjoyed listening to people's stories, especially in regard to the instances they recollect from their childhood. I take pleasure in interviewing folks and noting the events that have influenced them throughout their lifetime. I become absorbed in the moments of triumph and disappointments, cultural experiences, and chance encounters, which mold all of our lives, and these, are the tales I desire to convey.

Most of the stories I transcribe are from eras long gone—some from a few decades ago, and others from periods in time which have long been forgotten. As people tell me their stories, I delightfully visualize the specifics in my mind. I see their narratives like a movie reel shining on the silver screen. Therefore, when I agree to write a memoir for someone, I gather as many details as possible during the interview process, but there are certain particulars, which must be created to make the characters realistic and imaginable for the reader.

Many of the memoirs I have inscribed, such as *Molly's Memoir, Angels of the Appalachians, Erma's Attic,* and *Rosa's Castle* are composites of actual historical events with fictional elements intertwined throughout the chronicle. Such is the case with *Jinx at the Greenbrier*. These tales cannot be classified simply as fiction, nor can they be considered entirely nonfiction. The most accurate classification, I believe, would be creative nonfiction.

I am devoted to telling the story as accurately as possible while striving to make the characters and scenes interesting, vivid and lively for the reader. This is why one of my favorite quotes is by Rudyard Kipling, "If history were told in the form of stories, it would never be forgotten." *Jinx at the Greenbrier* is an example of this. It is a snapshot of an actual historical place and time, imparted in a fictional format.

With this being noted, I sincerely hope you enjoy reading about Jinx and her remarkable accounts of growing up at the grand Greenbrier Hotel in White Sulphur Springs, West Virginia.

Warm Regards,

Deanna Edens

Preface

I SLUNG MY jacket onto the faux leather couch and glanced around my new house. The open floor plan made it impossible to disguise the boxes that were still stacked in each corner of the dining area, and the black trash bags stuffed full of clothes haphazardly spilling out onto the freshly cleaned carpet. Sassy, my longtime feline friend, pawed at the dish on the floor, seemingly reminding me I was thirty minutes late and I hadn't filled her bowl in over three hours. I grabbed the bag of Pet's Pride and poured the poultry and seafood tidbits into the Mighty Mouse dish before examining the mail I had gathered from the mailbox at the end of the driveway. *Electric bill already?* I flung it on the table. *Vote yes for what?* I tossed it in the trashcan. An envelope with elegant handwritten lettering caught my attention. The United States Postal Service's yellow sticker designed for forwarding mail only marginally distracted me from the painstaking calligraphy work embellishing the stationery. I squinted in an attempt to examine the return mailing address, rummaged through my purse, and victoriously plucked out my reading glasses. *I don't know anyone named Jinx who lives in White Sulphur Springs, West Virginia.*

It was an invitation to stay, all expenses paid, at the luxurious Greenbrier Hotel for a week. The catch? It was nothing unreasonable, only to listen to and potentially write the memoirs of an eighty-six-year-old woman named Jinx. She explained that a mutual acquaintance, named Geneva Lacy, had loaned her a few of my previously published books, and this was why she had chosen to contact me. The woman indicated she had "lived" at the Greenbrier for over a decade, and spent every summer at the hotel after she left to attend college in 1948. Her mother had been the Tea Master for half a century and she had some stories she would like to convey. If I agreed to this proposition, she would meet me at the green-domed Springhouse at precisely four o'clock p.m., on the twenty-third of June. Compensation, in addition to staying at the world-renowned resort, would be four hundred dollars per day. She also specified that no RSVP was required. All I had to do was show up.

An all-expensive paid trip to the Greenbrier? I pondered judiciously. *I don't start work at the university until mid-August. My neighbor said she would gladly care for Sassy anytime if I would graciously return the favor when she traveled.* I looked down to see Sassy amble over to recline in a spot of sun shining through the sliding glass door. "Sassy, do you mind if I take a short vacation without you?" She didn't even twitch a whisker so I figured she didn't give a hoot one way or the other.

Why not?

I energetically began searching through the black plastic bags, which served as my luggage while moving, hoping to locate my finest pale pink poplin dress, my best pair of dress slacks, which were allegedly wrinkle-free, and my favorite non-iron Calvin Klein sleeveless blouse. I stumbled upon my sling back shoes I had been rifling for, along with my choker necklace with dripping beads.

Fully realizing I had little time to prepare for the trip, I wavered for a brief moment, mainly because I am a person who likes to plan in advance. The two-week delay, due to the mail being forwarded to my new address, meant I would have to get on the road tomorrow. *Should I go?* I shifted my weight as I thought out the proposal. *Absolutely.* I firmed my decision. *Greenbrier Resort, here I come.*

The pleasant weather gave way at midday. A sudden chill blasted over the Allegheny Mountains, sending thousands of leaves spiraling about in green and buttery whirls. Iron-gray clouds came sweeping over low, dragging their dark skirts over the hilltops. I pulled to the side of the curvy West Virginia back road and turned Justin Timberlake singing "Can't Stop the Feeling"

off before pressing the button to close the convertible top of my Mitsubishi Spyder. As soon as I latched the top, a downpour of rain dumped down on me like a bucket of grubby wash water being tossed from an upstairs window.

I waited a couple of moments for the deluge to cease. When it lightened up a fraction, I pulled back onto the narrow two-lane highway and crawled along, well below the posted forty-mile-per-hour speed limit. The cascade of rain started in again, and even though my windshield wipers were beating frantically at high speed, I could barely see three feet in front of me. It didn't appear there was a shoulder to pull off the highway, so I continued to edge forward at my decelerated pace.

The rain continued for over an hour as I slowly made my way along the pothole-covered trail I noticed that the mountain had newly developed streams with brown liquid whooshing down the crevices. I heard a rumble and glanced in my rear-view mirror. A mudslide had collapsed onto the road only ten yards behind me. "Oh, sweet Jesus." I started praying.

A deafening sound boomed. Seconds later, falling rocks tumbled down the steep hillside. Again, I stared into the rear-view mirror only to watch, in horror, as the bulky boulders tumbled, colliding chaotically down the vertical slope. The stones, I could see, had covered the entire roadway and the mound appeared to be as tall as a building. "Oh, dear Lord. I don't know if I have anything I need to confess, but please forgive me for anything I am unaware of and please get me out of this mess."

There was no going back now. All I could do was creep forward.

When I reached the pinnacle of the road I could see, to my right, the walls of water had lifted a mobile home and it was being carried alongside the edge of the swollen banks of the gurgling ravine. The thunderheads dominated the whole sky; they came sashaying across, their undersides lowering and dragging blankets of rain under them. I tapped on my brakes, vigilantly watching for overflow covering the highway. Panicking, I attempted to gauge the depth of the stream. No, it wasn't a stream now—it was a river—the embankments swollen and overflowing.

From this vantage point I could see the force with which the water moved and destroyed everything in its path. An automobile tipped up in a nauseating display of the raging river's power, and it began gliding along the surface. *Is there a woman caught inside the car?* My right hand fondled around inside my purse searching for my cellphone as the swirling flood-water, which was as thick as cake batter, demolished everything in a few seconds of roaring peril.

Suddenly, the bridge I was approaching, and needed to cross, tilted up on one end as the debris, which had piled high in the water, plunged into it, ripping it from its steel beams. The unstoppable force carried the chunks of concrete slab on its murky top as it continued to turbulently gush through the valley. I slammed on my brakes, my heart thumping violently, and saw a sign indicating that the Free Will Baptist Church was less than a mile down the road to my left. The cross on the sign seemed to glisten, providing me with a morsel of hope.

Turning sharply through the black creek, which had pooled at the mouth of the rutted hollow, I breathed a sigh of relief as my adrenaline rush subsided—then a realization hit me like a blow to my gut. *Flashflood.* The river was rushing ominously—muddy water was gushing down, swooshing tumultuously across my path. The rumbling, hissing force of the stream, mixed with debris and wreckage, was pounding against the driver's side door of my car.

Everything turned white as the sky cracked open along a convoluted cobalt-white seam. A tree flashed and exploded a few feet ahead and the bolt of noise triggered my head to whip forward. I could smell the tree burning—a fresh, strange scent filled the air—reminiscent of logs burning in an open fire pit.

Then the fragrant aroma of freshly baked chocolate chip cookies began drifting in the air…

I leisurely strolled around the edge of the perfectly manicured Croquet Lawn, where I anticipated I would see several men, dressed from head-to-toe in white, participating in a croquet outing. However, there were no sporting events taking place today.

Instead of the sun shining brightly and wispy clouds changing shapes overhead, dreary clouds shielded the sky and deep puddles saturated the cropped grass forcing me to step over and around them in order to avoid permanent damage to my suede Birkenstocks.

Sporting my best messy up-do and pale pink slip dress, I spotted the green-domed Springhouse. I glimpsed at my watch and was pleased to discover I was fifteen minutes early. I certainly didn't want to arrive late and risk forgoing the opportunity to meet Jinx, and if I were late she may naturally assume I had declined her invitation.

Unwrapping the napkin that protected the chocolate chip cookie I had pilfered from the hotel lobby, I leaned against a tall pillar and took a nibble. My attention was drawn to a lovely woman wearing a silk dress, who was trying to calm her fussy infant—milk spittle was dribbling down her back. Suddenly, as if appearing from nowhere, a very petite woman approached me. *This must be Jinx.* I tucked the half-eaten cookie back into its protective cover, dropped it into my purse, and quickly scrubbed my front teeth with my finger to make sure I didn't greet her with a cocoa-tainted smile.

"Are you Dee?" The woman's eyes crinkled up delightfully when she addressed me.

"Yes, and you must be Jinx." I offered her my hand.

"It is very nice to meet you." She shook my hand tenderly. "I am so happy you decided to come."

"Your letter was very intriguing," I admitted.

"I am so glad you made it. The flashfloods can be horrid this time of year."

I nodded in agreement. "The rainfall was treacherous and I was concerned I would be late for our meeting."

"Fortunately, you made it." Happy as a lark, she motioned toward a chair indicating that I should join her. "Geneva Lacy shared some of your books with me and I enjoyed reading them. I simply adore the method you use when writing biographies—the back and forth from the present to the past.

You make the story come alive." She smiled at me sincerely. "Your descriptions are very vivid."

"Thank you." I modestly replied.

Jinx got straight to the point. "I was hoping you would consider writing my memoir."

I took in a deep breath. "Well, to tell you the truth, I would love to try. However, I have to admit that sometimes I can't fully relate to the stories folks have shared with me and if I'm not able to picture the scenes in my mind…"

She laughed and nodded knowingly. "I completely understand." Jinx tucked a loose strand of her shortly bobbed hair behind one ear before tugging a green napkin from the pocket of her Armani wide-leg trousers. "Would you care for a chocolate chip cookie? I smuggled some out from the lobby."

I giggled as I reached into my purse and sheepishly exposed my own stash.

"You are a woman after my own heart." Her eyes smiled charmingly. "Let me tell you a story."

"Please do."

"My parents had only been married a short time before they were expecting me, and at the time, there were few jobs in Greenbrier County, so my papa had a friend who worked in the Bethlehem mine in Barracksville, West Virginia and he promised Papa he could get him a job working there. Now one of the worst jobs, possibly in the world, is being a coal miner. Nonetheless, Papa wanted to provide us with as nice of a life as he could, so my parents packed up their belongings and moved to the little town."

I pulled a mechanical pencil from behind my ear and began jotting details in my notepad.

"I don't recall much about living there, but Mama said the folks were kind and humble people. My mama was sort of a doctor in the town—unofficially, of course. She had learned to make healing tea, and the poor folks who lived there would often call on her when they had a fever or other conditions."

Jinx sighed deeply. "Mama told me the coal dust drifted around in the air constantly, and she could clean the small shack everyday, trying to erase the endless layer of black soot, which settled on furniture, trees, homes, and even the people, but it came back the moment she threw the rag back into the pail. She worried every day when Papa would head out to work that he may not come home, because less than ten years earlier an explosion occurred at the Bethlehem mine and thirty-three men lost their lives."

"Slow down a little, Jinx. I'm trying to capture the specifics."

She stopped talking and waited until I nodded my head, indicating I was ready to continue. "They moved to the tiny coal mining community in 1932 and on the twelfth day of May in 1935, my mama's nightmare became a reality. It was around midnight when Papa and Mama heard someone banging on the front door. My papa opened the door and we could hear him talking to Mr. Welty, who was a section boss."

I cringed, already knowing where this was leading. I had seen and heard horrid stories about the coal mining disasters and knew they never turned out favorably.

"'We've gotta a fire goin' on in the mine and we need some help puttin' it out,' he told my papa."

"'I'll be right there,' my papa promised as he slid on his shoes and coat." Jinx remembered, what seemed to be, a long lost detail. "He didn't bother to change out of his pajama bottoms."

"He put himself in danger to help others, right?" I presumed.

"He went to the mine. My mama pleaded with him. 'David, don't go. This isn't safe. No fire is worth riskin' your life over.'"

"So true," I mumbled.

"My papa was a responsible man, so he told my mama, 'I can't just not show up. What if there are men caught in the mine that need my help?'"

"I guess he was right in that respect." I realized, all the time doubting I could be so brave.

"Mama screamed at him. 'Don't go!' He whispered, 'I've gotta, sweetie.' He kissed my mama on the lips and gave me a tight hug before the door slapped shut behind him."

"What happened next?" I prompted, still hoping there was a happily ever-after ending.

"Mama started prayin' and she kept repeating the Lord's Prayer over and over again. It wasn't too long after he left that a deafening roar thundered across the valley. Flames shot five hundred feet into the air causing the whole sky to light up like fireworks on the Fourth of July. Mama picked me up and started running, barefoot, with nothing on but her thin nightdress, towards the shaft of the mine. People were scampering from all directions. Most had been awakened from sleep and seemed disoriented, unsure of the situation. I could hear low voices whispering as we approached the mouth of the mine. 'Who's down in the pit?' 'What are they doin' down there at this hour?' We waited and waited, shivering and crying, as anguished sobbing surrounded us. The crescent moon peeked through the thick clouds from time to time, but for the most part, only the occasional lantern flickering around the shaft of the mine was visible. Trepidation masked my mama's face as she waited—her hands wringing nervously. Eventually she stopped crying. I figured all her tears were used up."

I shook my head in sympathy. *I can't even imagine the fear her mama felt.*

"Then just as the sun crested above the mountaintop, the heartbreaking news came. Five men were burned to death and six others injured, when the miners, who were working with a hose to extinguish the flames, were burned by hot steam from the jets of water forcing back upon them when the walls of the shaft collapsed."

"I'm so sorry." I sincerely conveyed, fully aware I could never begin to fathom the terror.

Jinx paused for a moment, seemingly to collect her thoughts. "They advised my mama not to look at Papa. They told her it would be best to bury him in his casket without viewing the body. Nonetheless, she said she wanted to be sure. One man insisted she should only look at his hand and he had carefully removed the lower portion of Papa's left arm from underneath the black cloth covering his body. His silver wedding ring, which matched mamas precisely, was barely visible due to the swelling and blistering triggered by the scorching steam. She later confessed that she wished she wouldn't have looked, because the sight of his charred skin haunted her dreams forever."

"Did she forgive the man who had asked your papa to help contain the fire?"

"There was no need for forgiveness. It was Papa's choice to go down into the pit, plus Mr. Welty, the man who had knocked on our door on the fateful night, perished in the catastrophe alongside of my papa."

"Did you stay in Barracksville afterwards?"

"We didn't stay after the explosion. My mama buried my papa beside the other men who were killed in the mine and two days later she mailed a letter to her friend, Roy Sibert, asking if he would come and get us."

"Who is Roy Sibert?"

"Roy Sibert was my mama's friend. He had secured a job at the Greenbrier Hotel when he was seventeen. He didn't want to be a coal miner like his daddy was, so he had worked his way up from the night desk cashier to the executive suite of the luxury hotel. He had known my mama since she was knee-high to a grasshopper and had told her, before we moved off to Barracksville, that he would come and fetch us anytime we wanted to come home. And he was as good as his word. He came for me and Mama and we packed our scarce belongings in the trunk of his car and made the trip back to Greenbrier County. Roy found us a two-room house to rent and hired my mama to work in the kitchen at the Greenbrier Hotel." Jinx paused for a moment. "Actually, the folks who live around here call the Greenbrier the Old White. So if you hear someone refer to the hotel as Old White, it's because the names are used interchangeably in this neck of the woods."

"I may have read this information somewhere before," I replied as I searched through my memory bank, "or perhaps not. Sorry, please continue."

"Well, Mama started working here and since I had no one to stay with while she was working, Sibert—that's what everyone called Roy—told my mama I could come to work with her and stay in the kitchen area or play outside on the lawn. A five-year-old couldn't get into too much trouble, right?" She laughed good-heartedly. "Most all the folks who worked here spoiled me rotten. I was a very small child for my age and everyone thought I was intelligent due to my knack for carrying on conversations with adults. I believe it was because I spent a great deal of time around adults that I seemed mature for my age."

Petite frame and adult interaction. I wrote this down and circled it twice.

"My mama used to tell everyone that I was born old." A smile curved up around Jinx's cheeks, "Born old," she repeated, "I often wondered what she meant."

"Who owned the resort during this time?"

"The Chesapeake and Ohio Railroad purchased the resort in 1910."

"Was it as extravagant back then as it is now?"

"The resort was definitely highfalutin' even back then. Everyone who worked here dressed entirely in white. The waiters wore their starched white jackets and black bow ties. The finest flatware and silver coffeepots, and beautiful flowers adorned each table. The meals were cooked to perfection and folks came from all over the world to spend time here. The Greenbrier is widely regarded as one of the finest resorts in the world. It is also one of the most historical places in the United States. Having served as a Confederate hospital during the Civil War, it was frequented by Robert E. Lee after the war. It has housed high-level German and Japanese diplomats during World War II, served as a hospital for the duration of the war, maintained a top-secret bunker for high ranking officials of the United States, and served as a place to rest and vacation for the rich and famous for centuries. I have met hundreds of important and interesting folks. Some I was able to have lengthy conversations with, and others only fleeting encounters."

I could easily ascertain the joy Jinx felt when talking about this grand place. "So, Jinx, do you have some stories to tell me concerning the folks who stayed at the Greenbrier?"

Her brows wiggled conspiratorially, "Indeed, I have some tales to tell."

Tea with Eleanor

Tea with Eleanor
June 1936

"WOULD YOU KINDLY brew the First Lady a pot of tea?" Sibert requested.

"The President's wife is here? I had no idea." Jinx's mama replied. "Any particular type?"

"She didn't request anything specific, so the customary blend should be appropriate." He paused for a second. "Unless you determine otherwise." Sibert cleared his throat before continuing, and in a nearly apologetic tone of voice he asked, "Will you deliver the tray, too? Florence is not feeling well so I expect we'll be shorthanded all morning."

"It will be an honor." Jinx's mama, who was also known as the Tea Master, beamed as she smoothed a non-existent wrinkle from her crisply pressed white apron.

Six-year-old Jinx peeked her head out from a slit in the pantry door to listen in. *The President? I ain't ever met the President before.* Jinx silently slipped out of the lower cabinet, where she was playing with the Tailspin Tabby toy, which one of the maids had given to her after finding it abandoned in the lawn, and noiselessly followed her mama down the long hallway to room #145.

The fancy room right above the main entrance. Jinx approved. *A good choice.*

She watched her mama rap two times, wait for a response to come from within the room, open the door and quietly tender the serving tray onto the tabletop. "Please let us know if you need anything else."

"Thank you." The woman seated at the circular table replied with a polite smile.

Jinx darted behind the door before her mama turned to leave, and when the door soundlessly closed, she stood motionless staring at the tall woman. She knew the woman, who was studying a book, didn't know she had slipped into the room. She felt a sneeze coming on and covered her mouth in an attempt to mute the sound. It didn't work. The tea swooshed about in the woman's cup before splashing over the rim and dribbling onto her hand.

"Oh!" The lady stared at the child as she placed her cup of tea on the saucer, picked up her cloth napkin, and dabbed at the overspill. "Hello."

"Hello." The little girl dressed in lace replied.

A long hush followed. "Do you work here?"

"Nope. My mama does." She offered a further explanation, "I snuck in behind her when she was deliverin' your tea."

"I see." The lady smiled obligingly and Jinx noticed she had large protruding front teeth. "When I was a child I would pause quietly in the doorway, wanting to be acknowledged, and waiting to be asked in."

Jinx nodded. "Yep, that's what my mama tells me I'm supposed to do." Her eyes dropped to the floor. She studiously examined her toes before rocking back on her heels. "I don't always listen to my mama. I'll probably get a good scoldin' if she finds out."

"Sometimes a swift punishment is far better than a long scolding."

"For sure." The little girl tugged on the hem of her sleeve. "Can I ask ya somethin'?"

"Absolutely."

"Are you the President?"

"No, dear, I am the First Lady."

"The First Lady of what?" Jinx tilted her head.

"The First Lady of the United States of America."

Jinx's ears perked up with interest. "So you're more important than the President."

"No," the woman laughed, "however, my job is very important." She curiously studied the girl, who was wearing an oversized off-white lace dress. "Please, call me Eleanor."

"Pleased to meet ya, Eleanor. I'm Jinx."

"Jinx? What a delightful name." Her hand swirled welcomingly. "Would you like to join me for a cup of tea?"

"Okay." The little girl sauntered over and climbed up onto the tall chair.

Eleanor poured a cup of steaming tea and glided it across the table. "Be careful. It's very hot."

"Thank ya." Jinx gazed at the muffins and scones displayed on the porcelain-serving dish.

Eleanor nudged the plate toward the child so her guest could easily attain the goodies. "Please, help yourself."

Jinx chose a scone and smothered it with strawberry jam, as Eleanor took a long satisfying drink of the tea. "This is excellent tea."

"My mama made it. She's the Tea Master here. She can fix-up any kinda tea you'd want. She has recipes to help ya calm down, or to help ya quit hurtin'. She can fix anything ailin' ya."

"What a fine gift to possess!"

Jinx nodded. "She's smart and sweet, too."

"Tea always reminds me of my favorite saying—'A woman is like a tea bag, you never know how strong she is until she gets in hot water.'"

Grown-ups were always saying things that caused Jinx to stop and consider and this was no exception. "Do ya mean like takin' a bath?"

The First Lady's lips turned up in a half smile. "No," she sipped her tea, "it's more a reference to the strength women have when dealing with difficult situations. It's kind of like you never know what's in a person's heart until they are tested."

"Oh," Jinx responded, unaffectedly.

"Let me ask you something, Jinx. Do you have a mother-in-law?"

Jinx cautiously measured this. *I have a mama, and a grandma, and a pesky neighbor named Jack, who is always making stinker noises with his armpits. But I don't recollect havin' a mother-in-law.* She had overheard many folks at the Greenbrier complain about their mother-in-law but didn't recall ever meeting one. "I don't think so," she finally responded.

"You are lucky," Eleanor confided. "Are you married?" she asked in a teasing voice.

"No, I'm only six years old." The little girl smoothed the napkin on her lap.

"A very smart decision," the older woman replied.

"Yep," Jinx further expounded, "today is my birthday and I am six." She held up her right hand widely displaying her fingers, then licked the jam from her pointer finger of her left hand and stuck it up into the air.

"Well, happy birthday!"

"Thank ya." She fluffed her new hairpiece with her hand. "I got this bow for my birthday. Do ya like it?"

"It's beautiful."

"I didn't brush my hair this morning. Mama said I didn't have to if I didn't wanna, seein' how it's my birthday and all."

"Physical appearance is very overrated."

The small blond child tentatively nodded—completely unsure of what the woman meant.

"My mother-in-law once said to me 'If you would just run a comb through your hair, dear, you'd look so much nicer.'"

Jinx's jaw gaped open. "That wasn't a very kind thing to say."

"No, it wasn't polite at all."

"I'm sure glad I don't have a mother-in-law." The little girl carefully examined the woman. "Your hair looks just fine to me. Did ya run a comb through it this mornin'?"

"Not yet." Eleanor grinned before taking a big bite of blueberry muffin.

"Do ya remember when ya where six years old?"

"Only vaguely." She paused to remember, as she placed the muffin back onto the plate. "I was living in a convent in Paris at the time."

"Was livin' at a convent kinda like livin' at the Greenbrier?"

"Not even close." Eleanor poured herself some more tea before examining her guest's cup and topping it off with a splash. "I didn't stay there too long because I was forced to leave."

Jinx's eyes grew wide. "They booted out the First Lady?"

Eleanor smiled. "I wasn't the First Lady back then, and yes, they booted me out."

Jinx leaned in close and asked in a whisper. "What'd ya do?"

"I lied."

"Oh." Jinx offered a disappointed expression, like her mama did whenever she invented stories. "What'd ya lie 'bout?"

"I told the nuns I had swallowed a coin."

"That's a silly fib." The child pursed her lips.

"Yes, it was. I only did so because there was another little girl who had swallowed a coin and was being comforted by the nuns and I wanted their attention. You see, Jinx, when I was a child, people didn't pay much attention to me. I always wanted someone to notice me. Someone to think I was special."

Jinx considered this momentarily. "Everybody thinks you're mighty special now, so I reckon it worked out alright for ya."

"Yes," she nodded, "I suppose this is true. One can never predict where our journey will lead us."

Jinx tilted her head questioning. "What were ya reading when I came in the room?" She pointed to the burgundy book, all the time admiring the brandished golden clasp securing the pages.

"I was not reading. I was thinking about writing. This is a journal for writing down your thoughts and ideas. Have you ever seen one?" She plucked up the diary and handed it to Jinx. "I have a speaking engagement at three o'clock. I will be addressing the Chi Omega sorority and I was considering the most appropriate topic for my speech."

Jinx ran her hand over the embossed leather. "This is a fancy book." She gingerly placed it back onto the tabletop. "Did ya figure out what you're gonna tell 'em?"

"Not really."

"Ya could tell 'em 'bout your mother-in-law."

Eleanor's eyes sparkled mischievously as if she were truly considering this option. "No, I shouldn't share this information, because I believe great minds discuss ideas, average minds discuss events, and small minds discuss people." She tapped the silver spoon on the edge of her teacup. "So I think I will discuss human rights."

Human rights? She wasn't sure she had heard this term before. "Grownups talk 'bout all kinda things I don't understand."

"Grownups don't always understand what they are talking about either," Eleanor replied, not bothering to veil her criticism.

"Do ya get scared when ya have to talk to a lot of folks at one time?"

"A little, and sometimes my voice wavers when I speak to large audiences." She pointed her finger at the girl confidently and offered some advice, "Do one thing every day that scares you."

"Okay, Eleanor." Her shoulders straightened as she thought it all through. "I will." Jinx wiped the crumbs from her face with the sleeve of her dress. "Do ya have a bow to wear for your speech? 'Cause I was figurin' that if ya didn't, then ya could borrow my new polka dot bow and ya wouldn't even need to brush your hair."

Eleanor laughed out loud. "Thank you for offering but I don't think it would look as beautiful on me, as it does on you."

Jinx shrugged her shoulders. "Alrighty then." She peered around the elegantly decorated room. She had been in every single room in the Greenbrier, at one time or another, so the overstuffed sofa and massive pieces of dark brown furniture didn't impress her like it did some folks. "I'd best be gettin' along before my mama starts lookin' for me."

"If you are around at three o'clock you should attend my lecture."

"If it was snowin' and cold I would. But it's summer… and it's my birthday and all," she replied apologetically. "Ya understand, don't ya?"

"I understand completely." Eleanor assured.

"Plus, I have a joke I've been plannin' on." Her eyes grew wide with excitement. "Do ya know Sammy?"

Eleanor paused to consider. "No, I don't believe so."

"I've got a good trick to play on him today," she sputtered out between giggles, "he's gonna be mighty surprised."

"Sounds as if you are quite ornery," Eleanor teasingly assumed.

"Yep, that's why they call me Jinx."

"Jinx," Eleanor held up her finger, "wait one moment. I'd like to give you a birthday gift."

"Thank ya, Eleanor. But ya don't have to."

"I would like to give you my journal."

Jinx grinned. "I'm gonna be startin' school in the fall and I reckon I'll be learnin' how to write then."

"Perfect. Let me scribble a quick note." The First Lady picked up her Golden Herringbone fountain pen and opened the journal to the front page. She eloquently inscribed:

Happy sixth birthday, Jinx!
Thank you for joining me for tea.
Warmest Regards,
Eleanor Roosevelt
June '36

She presented the burgundy journal along with the fine fountain pen to the child. Jinx ran her finger over the leather-embossed book before tucking it under her arm. As she proudly strolled out the door she turned and said, "Eleanor, if ya see my mama please don't tell her I joined ya for tea."

Eleanor made a zipping motion across her lips. "I will never divulge our little secret to a soul."

"*The* Eleanor Roosevelt?"

"I wish I had realized the significance at the time. Had I been a little older, I would have attended Eleanor's lecture and spent every possible moment with her." Jinx shrugged her shoulders. "I was only six years old."

"I know quite a bit about Eleanor's life, certainly not as much as historians, but I remember reading a humorous quote one time referencing her honesty. The quote went something like this, 'If she tells you a rooster dips snuff, you can look under its wing and find the can.'"

Jinx laughed out loud. "She was an inspirational woman, for sure. President Harry Truman once referred to her as the First Lady of the World."

"She was obviously the First Lady when you had tea with her," I was trying to recall my knowledge of history, "then she served for several terms afterwards, right?"

"Anna Eleanor Roosevelt was the First Lady during the four terms that her husband, Franklin Delano Roosevelt, was in office. If I had to guess, I would say from 1933 until 1945. Afterwards, she served as the United States Delegate to the United Nations. She was also very controversial because she was so outspoken, particularly on her stance regarding racial issues." Jinx leaned in and confided, "She also publicly disagreed with her husband's polices, which was unheard of in those days."

"Is there anything unusual or particularly memorable that is not so well-known about her life?"

"There is one thing I have always remembered. You see, once I was old enough to realize how much she had done for our country, I read everything I could get my hands on concerning her and her life. She became my heroine, or I suppose I should say, the epitome of what I would strive to be."

"A good choice for a role model."

"Having lived my entire life in West Virginia, I was always particularly interested in the planned community she launched to help the families of unemployed coal miners. It was called Arthurdale. Eleanor had visited some families of homeless miners in Morgantown a few years before I met her." Jinx tilted her head thoughtfully before asking me, "Are you aware of the poor treatment of the coal miners in West Virginia? For example, they would toss women out of the company-owned homes only days after their husbands were killed in the many mining accidents. It didn't matter if they had children or not. The unwritten policy was very simple—somebody had to be working if you were going to live there."

"Yes," I replied, "I have been told horror stories about the pathetic conditions."

"Well, Eleanor was very affected by the visit. The miners she visited had been blacklisted following union activities, so she proposed a resettlement community at Arthurdale where they could earn a living by subsistence farming, creating crafts, and manufacturing work. There were approximately fifty houses built. Each of the homes had modern conveniences of indoor plumbing, steam heat and the promise of proper medical care. Unfortunately, she had hoped for a racially mixed community, but the miners voted and wanted to exclude black and Jewish miners. As you can imagine, this undoubtedly made her as mad as a calf with a barbwire tail."

"Funny." I interjected.

"Ultimately, it made her more outspoken on the issue of racial discrimination."

"Yes, I know she fought diligently to expand roles for women in the workplace and embraced the concept of civil rights for everyone."

"By the time she died in November of 1962, she was regarded as one of the most esteemed women in the world."

"She is still highly regarded."

"I would think she was the most influential woman in United States history," the elderly woman added.

"It must have been a great honor to have tea with her."

"She was very gracious."

A long silence followed as I wrote down the ideas I wanted to make sure I didn't forget. Finally, Jinx spoke. "Would you care for a taste of America's Favorite Morning Laxative?"

"What?" My nose scrunched up.

"The White Sulphur Springs water has been for sale all over the country since 1902. I think they quit selling it around 1942, but one of the main reasons why this place first became so popular is because of the healing waters of the springs. For years, visitors in the Springhouse practiced a daily ritual of drinking a cup to keep them healthy or to cure their ailments. There was a Resident Physician named Dr. Mooreman who came to work here back in the mid-eighteen hundreds. He claimed the mineral waters of White Sulphur Springs were the most highly medicated and efficient mineral water of its class in, perhaps, the entire world."

"Really? Do you mean right here? In *this* Springhouse?"

"My mama would sometimes use the water from this very Springhouse to brew her specialty tea. Usually, if someone needed to cleanse their body," Jinx filled two glasses full, "or in certain cases, when they had bumped their head." She handed a glass to me. "Bottoms up."

An Egg for Sam

An Egg for Sam
June 1936

JINX SPIED HER mama talking to the folks from Lewisburg who ran the 4-H clubs. "We will be purchasing as much of the prize beef and lamb that we can get our hands on," she told them, as Jinx tugged at her sleeve. "Wait until I finished talking, Jinx," she reprimanded her. Jinx let out a long sigh of resignation, cupped the egg she had swiped from the icebox where the dairy products were stored, and waited impatiently. Finally, the boring grown-up conversation regarding cows had come to an end.

"Jinx, I've told you time and time again not to interrupt adults when they are speaking to one another."

"I know." She flashed her broad green eyes at her mama. "Sorry."

"What can I help you with?"

"Do ya know where Sammy is?"

"You've already met Sammy?"

"Yep." She had immediately fallen in love with his quick wit and down to earth demeanor.

"I would guess he's out on the driving range."

As she took off running in the direction of the golf course, she could hear her mama call out, "Don't forget to meet us in the kitchen after tea is served this afternoon. We have important business to take care of."

Jinx could see Sammy long before he saw her. His shabby white shirt stood out like a calla lily in full bloom against the green hues of the mountains surrounding the range. She approached him from behind and paused for a moment underneath the pleasant shade of the tall oak tree. She peered out over the lush meadows and dark treetops. She could overhear Sibert talking to him. They were very loud.

"What happened out there?" Sibert asked Sam.

"It was an accident. I was on the fifth tee and let loose a good, straight drive. It was flying straight and high and it must have gone over three hundred and thirty yards because it ended up on the green. Well, it ended up smacking Bradley right on his rump."

Sibert cringed. "You hit a member of the C&O Board of Directors on his bootie?" He ran his fingers through his hair. "Geez."

"He was bending over to pick up his own ball. I wasn't aiming at him."

"Bradley called you an ill-mannered fairway sniper and is insisting you be fired."

"Did you tell him it wasn't my second shot?"

"I told him I doubted it was your second shot, and I knew you often drove the ball all the way to the green."

"What did he say?"

"He didn't believe me and wants to see a demonstration of your skills."

"When?"

"Tomorrow morning."

Jinx waited until Sibert left and counted to ten, twice, before stepping out from her hiding place. "Hi, Sammy, what ya doin'?" She noticed he was barefoot. His shoes were tucked neatly on the ground beside his bag.

"Hey there, Jinx. I'm getting ready to practice my swing. Do you want to watch?" He bent over and selected a golf ball from a wire pail sitting on the ground to his side.

"Sure," Jinx said as she was figuring out a way to slip the egg into his bucket of balls. "Hey, look there!" She pointed in the direction of the clubhouse.

"What?" He turned and looked.

She bent over and carefully placed the egg on top of the pile of balls. "Oh, shucks. I thought I saw an elephant."

"An elephant?" Sammy shook his head. "You're one crazy kid, do you know that, Jinx?"

"Yep, and today is my birthday."

"Really? Well, happy birthday, Jinx."

"Thank ya. Let me ask ya somethin', why ain't ya wearin' your shoes?"

He wiggled his toes. "I like playin' barefoot."

"Don't it hurt your feet to walk 'round all the time without shoes on?"

"Nah, I could stomp a chestnut burr and not feel a thing."

She thrust her new journal toward him. "Eleanor gave me this book for my birthday. Would ya like to write somethin' in it?"

"Books are for readin', Jinx. Not for writin' in."

"This is a special book. Eleanor wrote something in it this mornin'."

"Alrighty then." He accepted the leather-bound book and fancy pen from the child's hands and as he opened it to the front page he saw the signature of Eleanor Roosevelt. "You had tea with Eleanor Roosevelt?" His jaw gaped open.

"Yep. How'd ya know?"

"She wrote a note in here."

"I know," Jinx rolled her eyes. "I don't start school until fall so I can't read yet." She looked over Sammy's shoulder. "What'd she write?"

"Eleanor wrote, 'Happy sixth birthday, Jinx. Thank you for joining me for tea.' Then she signed her name."

Jinx nodded. "She's my friend."

"You must be luckier than a cat with ninety lives—hobnobbin' with such important folks."

"Everybody's important, Sammy," she reminded him.

"I reckon so." Sammy paused for a moment, as if he were considering what to write. He bent down, placed the journal on his knee, and scribbled:

Happy birthday to my friend, Jinx.
I hope you're always as lucky as a cat with ninety lives.
Sam Snead
June '36

He handed it back over to her before seizing a ball. The little girl expectantly watched his hand.

Shucks.

"Look at this." He chose a long iron, started humming "The Merry Widow Waltz" and smashed the ball. They both shielded their eyes from the sun as it powered down the field. "How far do you think that one went? It bounced on a good roll."

"I don't know," Jinx replied, "better try another one."

"Yep, you're right. This might be the last time I get to hit a few smokers at the Greenbrier."

"You're last time? Ya just started workin' here this week," Jinx reminded him.

"I know. Unfortunately, I hit Mr. Bradley in the hind end this mornin', and he's madder than a mule chewin' on bumblebees."

"Why'd ya hit him?"

"I didn't mean to."

"Did ya tell him you were sorry?"

"Yep, I told him I was danged sorry. But," he sighed, "he didn't believe me. He wanted to cut me up like catfish bait. Mr. L. R. Johnston pulled Mr. Martin into the clubhouse and called him on the carpet. He said Mr. Bradley wanted them to fire me."

Jinx gasped, "They didn't fire ya, did they?"

"I got one more chance tomorrow. I'm gonna play a round with Mr. Bradley to prove to him that I can knock a drive three hundred and thirty yards. If I don't, I'm gonna lose my job making forty-five dollars a week, then I'll be back home waitin' for Ma to round us up on Sunday like she's callin' for the hogs, and I'll be eatin' brush rabbit and squirrel soup again."

"Where's your Ma live, Sammy?" Jinx asked.

"I grew up in the Back Creek Mountains where the valleys are so narrow that the dogs have to wag their tails up and down."

Jinx started laughing. "You're funny, Sammy."

"I don't feel very funny today. If I don't put on a show tomorrow, I'll be outta here by noon."

"I'll have mama fix ya up some of her special tea. The kind that gives ya power."

"That'd be fine. I can use all the help I can get." He pulled out his number one driving wood. "See this?" He pointed toward the cast-off head. "It's glued together. I tried to cover it up with a decent glaze and by rubbing shellac and linseed oil on it, but it ain't nothin' compared to what the other folks around here have in their bag. Maybe I don't belong in this fancy place."

"That don't matter," Jinx assured him. "Plus, Mr. Fred Martin is a good man."

Sammy nodded. "For sure. He's the one who offered me this job, and I'd hate to disappoint him." Sammy leaned on his club. "Do you know when he offered me this job I thought he was joshing me. Then I realized he wasn't. I told him that by the time he got back to the pro shop, I'd be the first thing he saw when he arrived." Sammy reached into the bucket, briefly grabbed the egg before setting it back down, and grasped another golf ball.

Shucks. Jinx thought. *When is he gonna grab the egg?*

Smack!

"There goes a straight, long lick," he said.

Jinx lost sight as it barreled down the field. "I think it curved a little bit."

"Why did I duck hook that shot?" He mumbled under his breath.

"Just give it another try."

Sammy bent down and drew out the egg.

He's got it this time. A big smile formed on her face.

He rolled the egg around in his hand a few times before placing it on the ground. "I'm gonna knock this one long," he crowed.

Sammy pulled his iron up above his shoulder, paused for a second, and forcibly swatted the egg. The shell cracked, egg whites sprayed, the yolk splattered high up into the air and all over his trousers.

Jinx started cackling like a hen—her amusing laughter echoing across the lawn. She was smacking her leg in a fit of hilarity when Sammy turned to face her. His brow teasingly narrowed. "Jinx!"

She turned and darted toward the protective walls of Old White, giggling all the way.

"I'm going to get you!" she heard him call out.

I'm gonna marry that man when I grow up. She was speculating as she pushed open the kitchen door.

"So, you were friends with Sam Snead?"

"For years I was in love with Sam Snead. It nearly broke my heart when he married Audrey. I told her at their wedding reception I was heartbroken when I learned he was going to marry her." Jinx smiled at the memory. "Audrey said, 'I'm just glad you're not ten years older or I would have some stiff competition.' That's when I played my last card. I asked her, 'Audrey, did you know Sammy likes to eat squirrel soup?' Her nose crinkled up disgustedly. 'You could have told me this *before* I married him.' She pulled me close and whispered, 'I'll take good care of him, Jinx. I promise.'"

"That is a touching story—very sweet." I acknowledged.

Jinx turned to face me. "Audrey was a fine woman and a good wife to Sammy."

"So he stayed working at the Greenbrier after the incident with Mr. Bradley?"

"After Sammy and Mr. Bradley played a round of golf together, Bradley hired Sammy for a coach. They worked together all summer, and when Mr. Bradley paid him at the end of the session, he told Sam to go buy some new clubs, but there were other things Sam needed more. He bought an old tin lizzy jalopy with a push horn on it that went 'kee-haw.' Every time I heard him blast the horn I went running to find him."

"I've heard a lot about Sam Snead, but I don't know many details regarding his life," I told the elderly woman.

"Sammy had a good career, a good marriage, and served in the war from 1942 until 1944. I was sure glad when he made it home safely."

"What else do you remember about him?"

"I remember after my mama brewed him his first cup of Oolong tea he asked for it every day," she explained, "it helps one concentrate. It works like a stimulant."

"Oh. Very interesting. I know virtually nothing about tea."

"I had asked mama to fix him up a cup the morning he was going to play Mr. Bradley. I hoped it would help him keep his job."

"Fortunately, he did, eh?"

"His game of golf was brilliant and he was allowed to stay on." A lopsided smile formed on her lips. "Sammy was very kind and possessed great dignity. For example, he told me when he was a child he and his older brothers had snuck away from Bible class and spent the morning repairing some old golf clubs. He was walking up the road swinging at dried up horse turds and rocks and one of the rocks took off like a bullet, went through a window at the church and sprayed glass all over the folks sitting in the pews. It wasn't too difficult to determine, considering the size of the congregation, who was missing Sunday service, but he ran into the woods and hid and nobody could ever prove he was the one who shot the rock through the window. Then, years later, when he had a little money, he purchased the Ashwood Methodist Church a new electric pipe organ. He said it was like a sinner who came to repent. What surprised me was he felt bad enough about the mishap that he set it straight, even though it was years after the incident had occurred."

"Honorable," I mumbled.

"We always kept in touch and he became the head pro here at the Greenbrier, after he came home from the war. He won many championships and was inducted into the Virginia Hall of Fame in 1973. Which, by the way, I attended."

"Is he still alive?"

A sad expression crossed Jinx's face. "Slammin' Sammy passed away in 2002. He was four days shy of reaching his ninetieth birthday when he died."

I reached over and patted her hand.

"Slammin' Sammy was my first love," Jinx whispered.

Inspiration for Clare

Inspiration for Clare
June 1936

———— ❦ ————

JINX BOUNCED INTO the salon to check on Susan. "Hi, Susan, how are ya today?"

"I'm doing fine. How about you?"

"Pretty good." The little girl started flipping through the magazines scattered on the table. "Did ya get any new magazines in today?"

Susan darted over to the table, snatched up the *True Detective Mysteries* magazine and tucked it under her arm.

"Susan," Jinx shook her head, "ya don't have to hide magazines from me. I can't read yet. I'm only lookin' at the pictures."

"I am fully aware of this." Susan told her as she placed the magazine on her workstation.

"Mama wanted me to check and see if ya wanted some tea?"

"I don't think so, but thanks for asking."

"Alrighty then." Jinx plopped down and skimmed through the latest copy of *Life* magazine, as she listened to the gossiping women who were having their hair styled. She quickly grew bored and decided to visit the front desk to find out who was checking in the hotel on this stunning day in June.

Sporting a stylish pink skirt with a single pleat in the front, a white sweater, and a matching cap with a little pink flower fastened on its rim, Clare Boothe Luce strolled to the front desk. Jinx noticed the fashionable cap was tilted slightly and nestled on her blonde, softly waved hair perfectly. "Reservations for Mrs. Luce," she announced as her eyes darted around the room. Her gaze stopped on a gold and cream French telephone. "A dazzling new fashion," she pointed toward the elaborate telephone.

"Yes, ma'am." The gentleman behind the desk replied without looking up. "We have you staying in the Virginia Wing, where you will see the work of William Grauer, who is in the process of illustrating the history of White Sulphur Springs from its humble beginning to its current status. The murals he is creating are not quite finished but they are divine. I hope you find it suitable."

"I am sure it will be fabulous," she replied with a wide smile that flashed pearly, albeit slightly crooked teeth.

Jinx paid particular mind to her extraordinary translucent skin and blue eyes, which seemed to shimmer, and watched in awe as she removed a white handkerchief and polished a pair of fuchsia-rimmed spectacles. The bellhop silently swept in and lifted away her burdens. Jinx followed behind as the tall man wheeled eight pieces of rose-colored luggage through the cavern of dozens of closed doors to Mrs. Luce's assigned room. The moment he left Jinx knocked on the door.

"Yes?" Clare peeked through the cracked door.

"Hello, Mrs. Luce. My name is Jinx, and I was just wonderin' if ya needed anything?"

"Do you work here?"

"No, but my mama does." She smiled. "I saw ya down there in the lobby when ya came in and figured ya were the prettiest lady I've ever seen."

"Thank you."

Clare patiently waited for the little girl to continue.

"Do ya know your lipstick, eye glasses, and fingernails are the same color?"

"I do. I planned it this way."

Jinx delicately fingered her pink hairpiece. "They almost match my bow."

"I see." The woman nodded.

"Today's my birthday," Jinx puffed up, "and I was hopin' ya might wanna write something in my special book." She shoved her new journal through the slightly ajar door.

Mrs. Clare Boothe Luce flung the door open. "Would you like to join me for a moment?"

"I surely would."

Clare motioned toward the green floral chair and when Jinx was comfortably seated she dropped down into the chair across from her. She unhitched the clasp, picked up a writing pen, and opened the journal to the first page. Her eyes grew wide. "You had tea with Eleanor Roosevelt this morning?"

"I surely did. She's my friend."

"Oh," was all she could manage to mutter. Finally, she admitted. "I hope to meet Mrs. Roosevelt someday."

"Ya outta call her up."

The beautiful lady started laughing so hard that it became infectious, and Jinx started giggling along.

"So," the little girl finally broached, "what are ya doin' here at the Greenbrier?"

"I am staying for three days and plan to complete a first draft of a play." She kicked off her shoes and leaned back in the overstuffed chair.

"What ya gonna write 'bout?"

Clare's smile quickly disappeared. "I'm not quite sure. I've been rolling some ideas around in my mind but haven't been able to settle on anything."

"Ya could write 'bout mother-in-laws." Jinx suggested. "Eleanor was tellin' me 'bout her mother-in-law this mornin'." She sighed melodramatically. "I don't have a mother-in-law and I'm dang sure glad I don't. Did ya know Eleanor's mother-in-law told her she would look prettier if she would just run a comb through her hair? I didn't think that was a very kind thing to say to somebody. Do you?"

"No, it was downright rude."

"Yep. I overhear all kinds of folks saying rude things 'round here. They don't know I'm listenin' in. Just this mornin' I heard two ladies, who are visiting from New York City, talkin' in the hair salon. They were sayin' somethin' awful 'bout a woman named Joan, and do ya know when Joan walked into the room they waved at her and said 'Hello, Dear Joan.' Then they just smiled like they hadn't been sayin' bad stuff 'bout her."

"Some women are malicious," Clare admitted, "unfortunately."

Jinx wasn't sure what malicious meant, but could tell by the way it rolled off Mrs. Luce's tongue it wasn't good. "My mama ain't." She assured. "She's the Tea Master here at the hotel. Maybe she could fix ya up a cuppa tea to help ya figure out what to write 'bout."

"Actually," Clare's finger rose into the air, "a brilliant idea just popped into my head. I think I will write on the subject of women. Yes, I will write lacerating portraits of spoiled New York socialites in beauty and exercise salons. I will take shots at every female stereotype imaginable." She started talking faster and louder as the ideas rolled through her mind. "The wealthy women, aristocratic upper-class women, secretaries, models, maids, cooks, and of course, happy wives and unhappy wives will all be included."

"Sounds fine." Jinx agreed.

"This is genius!" Clare rose suddenly and began to pace around the room. "Jinx, do you have any idea how much courage it takes to be a woman in today's society? To not bow down to the conventional characteristics men have assigned to us?"

"No, ma'am. I don't even know what courage means." She started picking at her fingernail, as she so often did when the adults started talking about boring things. "Grown-ups say all kinds of things I don't understand. But I reckon that's 'cause I'm six years old."

"Courage is to be brave and daring. It is to have the guts to try new things."

"I try new things all the time." She offered up a wide smile. "Did I tell ya today is my birthday?"

Clare suddenly froze. "How rude of me! Happy birthday! I nearly forgot. I still need to write something in your special book."

Jinx handed her the fountain pen, which Eleanor had bestowed to her.

"Did Eleanor give you this Golden Herringbone pen?" Clare asked, as she examined it closely.

"Yep, she sure did."

"It is a fine writing utensil and very valuable. Make sure you take good care of it," she advised as she placed the leather-embossed journal on the table:

For Jinx,
Thank you for the inspiration.
Always remember that courage is the ladder on which all other virtues mount.
Clare Boothe Luce
June '36

"Here you go, darling," Clare tendered her the journal, "and I have a special gift for you, as well." She removed her cap and detached the little pink flower fastened on its rim before presenting it to the child. "This will match your bow perfectly."

"Well, thank ya, Mrs. Luce." Jinx beamed.

"Please call me, Clare," the woman commented as she fastened the flower into the little girl's hairpiece, "after all, we are friends now, right?"

"Yes, ma'am. We sure enough are."

"Hey, Jinx," Clare proposed, as the child was walking out the door, "on second thought, would you ask your mama to brew me up some tea for creativity?"

"I surely will. Somebody will bring ya up a pot shortly."

"So you were the one who inspired Clare Boothe Luce to write the play *The Women?*" I asked disbelievingly.

"I may have contributed to the writing of the play, *The Women*. Well, my mama's tincture of Green tea with Ginseng may have helped a little, too. Whatever it was, I do know Mrs. Luce wrote the first draft of her most enduring play, *The Women*, during that three-day stay at the Greenbrier in 1936. The film version, which was produced in 1939, was a legendary smash. It starred Norma Shearer, Joan Crawford and Rosalind Russell. The play has been revived on Broadway and many times in academic, regional and community theaters." Jinx informed me casually.

"Do you know if she ever met Eleanor Roosevelt?"

"Later, at the onset of the war, Clare had accompanied her husband to a private dinner with President Roosevelt and the First Lady. I have also read that Mrs. Roosevelt had seen Clare's satire called *Kiss the Boys Goodbye* and had publicly predicted that she would become a first-rate playwright someday. She had also added, 'When the bitterness of the experiences which she has evidently had are completely out of her system.' I have no idea if this is true or not, but I have often wondered, when Clare and Eleanor dined together, if they discussed the cute little girl at the Greenbrier." Jinx let out a boisterous laugh while nudging me. "Just kidding."

"Did Clare Boothe Luce go into politics?"

"Mrs. Luce was quite outspoken in the political arena. She won the Republican seat in the United States House of Representatives and served as the United States Ambassador to Italy and Brazil. President Reagan awarded her the Presidential Medal of Freedom in 1983, and she was the first female member of Congress to ever receive this prestigious award."

"She was a writer and a public servant," I murmured, wondering how she could find the time to be so diversified.

"Naturally, I followed her remarkable career."

I started counting the years in my mind. "I would assume she has passed away by now."

"Clare died of brain cancer in 1987." She pointed her finger at me, "Folks don't understand everything she did for this country. She was truly a gifted, classy, and determined woman who made great strides for feminists."

The very moment Jinx cracked open the door leading to the kitchen, she heard her mama call out, "Jinx! Come here right now."

She could tell she was in trouble for something. "I need to tell ya somethin', Mama."

"Okay."

"Mrs. Luce would like a pot of tea to help her be creative. I think that's the word she said. Yes, creative was the word." Jinx proudly announced, hoping this would distract her mama from the scolding coming her way. The little girl had no idea which of her pranks had been discovered and fully realized she could never tell which way the pickle was gonna squirt. She held her breath in anticipation.

"Fine. I'll send a pot of tea up to her." Her mama propped her hand on her hip. "Young lady, you need to get yourself down to the porter's room and apologize to Martin. Right now!"

"What do I need to tell him I'm sorry 'bout?" She intensely examined the toes of her shoes.

"There was an incident involving a tree frog in his hat this morning."

Jinx looked perplexed.

Her mama arched her brow. "It nearly scared the bejeebers out of him when it started hopping around on his head."

Jinx started laughing hysterically and smacked her knee joyfully. "Did the frog stay in there all that time? Well, I'll be."

Her mama pointed to the door with great fury and told her in no uncertain terms, "Now!"

The little girl scampered to the lowest cabinet in the pantry and tucked the new book that Eleanor had presented to her into her special hiding place. She meandered out the kitchen and down the long corridor leading to the porter's office. She cracked the door open and peeped around the corner. "Martin? Are ya in here?"

"I am." She heard a stern voice coming from behind a tall cabinet. "I've been waiting for you." He put his cap on the hat rack, like he always did, and told Jinx he had some serious business to discuss.

"Martin," she compressed her lips to keep from laughing, "I'm so sorry 'bout puttin' that tree frog in your cap this mornin'."

"So, it *was* you." His eyes narrowed.

"Yep," she responded in a lackadaisical manner, "I thought ya liked frogs."

"I do," he glared at her intently, "but I don't like them jumping around underneath my cap when I am doing my job. When Mrs. Luce arrived this afternoon, I went to open her car door and felt the little amphibian bouncing up and down. It croaked, Jinx. It croaked out loud! Can you imagine what Mrs. Luce thought when she heard croaking sounds coming from the porter?"

"She probably figured ya were lettin' out a stinker." She started giggling. She tried to stop but couldn't help herself.

"Come with me, young lady. We are going to have a talk with your mama."

Her shoulders drooped dispiritedly. This was it. She would never live to see her seventh birthday. "Oh, do we have to?"

He waggled his finger. "Follow me."

She disconcertingly shuffled behind Martin down the long hallway. He pushed open the kitchen door and pointed, indicating she should enter first. With her head hanging low she stepped over the threshold.

"Surprise!" She looked up to see Sibert, her mama, Sammy, Ms. Alice, the maid who would give her things other children had left behind at the hotel, Roberto, the head chef, Freddie, who was the desk cashier during the day, and of course, Martin, who had followed her through the door.

"A surprise?" Her hands rose to cover her heart. "Is it for my birthday?"

"Yep." Roberto presented her with a birthday cake, which held six pink spiraling candles.

"Oh, my goodness. How'd ya'll know today was my birthday?"

"You may have mentioned it in passing," Sammy reminded her.

Her mama lit the candles as everyone settled around the tall table. Jinx jumped up on a chair, grinning from ear to ear.

"You need to make a birthday wish before you blow out your candles." Sibert told her.

"There are a whole lot of candles on the cake, Jinx. You're gonna have to take a big breath to blow them all out, so you better be careful 'cause you might pass out cold from takin' in all that air at once," Sammy advised.

Jinx inhaled deeply then exhaled with great force. Splatters of spittle sprayed all over the spiraling candles.

Sibert cringed. He ran his fingers through his hair. "Geez."

Jinx's hand rose to her forehead. "I'm feelin' faint." She hopped down from the chair. "I think I used up all my air." She clutched her throat. She twirled around and around in circles. "This is it." She dropped to the floor.

Her body convulsed, she was shaking uncontrollably. Suddenly she went limp. One last agitated jerk trembled through her body before she wilted, lifelessly on the floor.

Silence filled the room.

"I told her not to take in all that air." She heard Sammy say to the others.

"Well," Sibert sighed, "she's a goner now."

Martin suggested, "We may as well eat her birthday cake since she won't be able to enjoy it."

"So true."

Her mama joined in. "I'm gonna miss her, but I reckon I could have a tiny sliver in her honor."

Jinx opened one eye. "Ya'll ain't eatin' my birthday cake without me." She sprang up and climbed back onto the tall chair before grinning at everyone in the room. "Thank ya'll for the birthday party."

"So, let me get this straight. On your sixth birthday you had tea with Eleanor Roosevelt, played a trick on Sam Snead while he was practicing on the golf range, inspired Clare Boothe Luce to write her award winning play *The Women,* and had birthday cake at the Greenbrier?"

"It's been exactly eighty years since I celebrated my sixth birthday here at the Greenbrier, and I will never forget it."

"I won't forget it either. It is an amazing story."

"It was a most memorable day."

"Did you keep asking people to sign the autograph book Eleanor gave to you?"

"For years I would stop people as they were walking through the lobby, or out on the grounds, and ask them for an autograph. Most of them would simply smile and scribble down their signature, but there were some people who engaged in conversations with me. The folks I chatted with were, of course, more memorable than those I met in passing. Over the years I managed to get signatures from George Marshall, Prime Minister Nehru of India, Ben Hogan, John F. Kennedy, President and Mrs. Nixon, Lyndon Johnson, and Prince Rainier and Princess Grace—just to name a few."

"Wow. I bet your book is worth a fortune."

"I would never sell my beloved autograph book. It encompasses my fondest memories."

"I understand. However, I would love to see it sometime."

Jinx nodded in agreement before continuing. "Let me tell you the stories of some of the more memorable celebrities I was fortunate enough to spend time with. These are the memories I have captured in my mind." Jinx tapped at her forehead. "The interactions I will never fail to recall."

"Great, I'm ready." I found my pen and notebook and prepared to take notes. "Let me ask you something, Jinx. You were obviously an ornery child. Did you ever grow out of it?"

"I am eighty six years old and still as curious and rebellious as I ever was."

The War

The War
December 1941

On a quiet afternoon, on the seventh day of December in 1941, while the folks were seated around the bar at the hotel, listening to the ballgame between the Giants and the Dodgers, the war struck home. A dispatch from the White House interrupted the programming and informed the citizens of the United States of America that the Japanese had attacked Pearl Harbor. Three days later Germany and Italy declared they were also at war with the United States.

Ten days after the attack on Pearl Harbor, Sibert was in the room when the General Manager, L.R. Johnston, received a cryptic telephone call from the State Department. Sibert's face was as white as a sheet when he opened the door to the kitchen and sat at the table where Jinx, her mama, Sammy, and Martin were feasting on egg salad sandwiches and sweet tea for lunch.

"President Roosevelt has ordered the removal of all enemy diplomats from the capital within forty-eight hours. They want us to accommodate the diplomats and their families from the newly hostile nations here." He glanced around at the concerned faces. "Since we are relatively isolated they believe we can be guarded easily."

"They're gonna need some kind of guards. The folks around here aren't gonna be too keen on puttin' up the enemies here at the Greenbrier." Sammy offered his opinion. "This whole thing is just crazy. I've been thinkin' about joinin' the military. This is America, we can't stand by and let other countries bomb us." He stood up and started pacing around the room.

"I think the idea is if the foreigners are treated favorably, then our diplomats will also be treated satisfactorily until they can figure out what's what."

"I think you should call the staff together and let them know what's goin' on." Jinx's mama suggested.

"Yep." Sibert ran his hand through his hair. "Geez."

Eleven-year-old Jinx, who was always thinking ahead, asked Sibert, "Will the children have to go to school? If they don't have to go, I ain't goin' either."

"Jinx," her mama scolded, "Sibert has more serious problems to deal with right now."

"She's right," Sibert deliberated briefly, "we'll convert some of the cottages in Georgia Row to classrooms so the school-aged children will be able to attend school."

"So," Jinx's eyes grew wide, "I can go to school here, too?"

Sibert sighed, "I don't know yet."

On December nineteenth, one hundred and sixty German and Hungarian diplomats arrived on a Pullman train from Washington, D.C. They came in looking like any other guests, wearing fur coats, and carrying dozens of bags and bundles. The FBI and United States Border Patrol arrived at the same time. The hotel was closed to regular guests and in no time things changed at the Greenbrier. It was now a private luxury resort and the focal point of international wartime diplomacy, and Jinx enjoyed every moment.

She immediately made friends with Aliz, Benci, Albert, and Marianna, whose father was a Hungarian diplomat, and they spent many hours swimming and splashing one another in the indoor pool.

It was exactly five days after the Hungarians moved into the Greenbrier Hotel, that the most exciting day in the world finally arrived. It was Christmas Eve. Jinx and her new friends were seated around a small Christmas tree they had decorated in the corner of the recreation area. Marianna explained to Jinx that in Hungary, Christmas, or St. Mikulás Day, was celebrated on the sixth day of December. On the night before St. Mikulás Day children would leave their polished boots outside the window. If the children had been good over the year, St. Mikulás would fill their boots with treats, chocolates, peanuts, and books, but if they had been naughty they would wake up to find the boots stuffed full of twigs.

"Twigs?" Jinx's jaw plunged open, as visions of branches, sticks and brushwood jam-packed in her rubber boots flashed through her mind. "I've heard of Santa Claus leaving lumps of coal for naughty children but never twigs."

"It's true." Albert assured, adding an exaggerated nod of his head.

"Well, here in America Santa Claus will visit us tonight, which is Christmas Eve." She opened a book that Mrs. Jones, her schoolteacher, had allowed her to borrow. "Let me read ya a book." She sat in a chair and twisted to display the pictures to her friends, just like Mrs. Jones did when she was reading to her class at school. "'Twas the night before Christmas, when all thro' the house, not a creature was stirring, not even a mouse." She continued to entrance her friends with the colorful illustrations and rhyming lines as she turned each page.

Just as she was reciting the last line, "But I heard him exclaim, ere he drove out of sight—Happy Christmas to all, and to all a good night," Santa Claus suddenly appeared in the room. "Ho! Ho! Ho! Merry Christmas!" Jinx, Aliz, Benci, Albert, and Marianna gasped in unison before Jinx let out a screech of delight. Jinx took off running toward him with her friends following behind. "See," she pointed to the man dressed in red, "what'd I tell ya'll?"

Santa encouraged the children to sit on his lap and tell him what they hoped to get for Christmas and presented each of them when a candy cane and a box wrapped in white paper with a large red bow ornamenting the top. They tore into the boxes and wrapping paper went flying chaotically through the air. Jinx squealed again as she held her new pink striped pajamas close to her chest. "I love new pajamas." She rubbed the soft cotton fabric on her cheek. "I always get a new pair of pajamas on Christmas Eve, 'cause on Christmas morning my mama always borrows a camera from Mr. Johnston and takes a photo of me opening up my Christmas present." Her eyes grew wide with excitement. "We could have Mama take a picture of all of us, right now. I'll ask her." She started jabbering out orders, "Ya'll go put on your new pajamas and meet me by the huge Christmas tree in the main lobby." She looked from one attentive pair of eyes to another. "I think this is a perfect idea."

She turned to face Santa and pointed her finger at him. "Meet us in fifteen minutes by the Christmas tree." She leaned in and whispered in his ear, "I figure Sibert is gonna need to get his shoes back from ya shortly. His feet are probably gettin' cold."

Aliz, Benci, Albert, and Marianna scampered off to change into their new pajamas and Jinx scurried into the kitchen to fetch her mama. She shoved the door open. "Mama, come and take a picture of us by the Christmas tree. I need to change into my new pajamas."

"Where did you get new pajamas?"

"Santa visited us in the recreation room."

"Really? How exciting." She picked up the Leica camera she had borrowed from Mr. Johnston. "It was very generous of Santa to visit the Greenbrier on Christmas Eve, because tonight is his busiest night of the year."

"Mama," Jinx propped her hand on her hip, "it's not the *real* Santa."

"How do you know?"

"He's wearin' Sibert's shoes."

"Oh." Her mama whispered, "Did you tell your friends?"

"Of course not, Mama. I don't want to ruin it for 'em."

A few minutes later, Jinx and her friends were posing in their new pajamas, underneath the eight-foot-tall Christmas tree as the lights twinkled and blinked, spraying glimmers of red prisms throughout the room. The jolly Santa Claus chortled out one last, "Ho! Ho! Ho!" before whispering into Jinx's ear. "I need to get Sibert's shoes back to him and change back into my dirty boots. Sibert told me I couldn't come into the Greenbrier with mud splattered on my boots."

"Really?" Jinx gulped. "Well, I'll be."

The children spent many happy months gallivanting around the estate, and although the golf course and riding trails were off limits, due to security concerns, Jinx showed them where the Ping-Pong table was set up, the best place to find tree frogs, and how to make a homemade fishing pole to use in Howard's Creek, if they could manage to get off the grounds.

One afternoon, in mid-March, when the trees were just beginning to burst forth the fresh new shades of spring, and the air smelled as crisp as summer rain, Jinx and her friends decided to have lunch out by Howard's Creek. The creek lies below the Old White's first tee, and is snuggled low underneath the soaring mountains. Her mama had packed them a picnic lunch, which included strawberry jam sandwiches, celery sticks, and sugar cookies, and Jinx propped her new slouch fedora hat, which Ms. Alice had found and ultimately given to her, on her head. Her friends followed her as she snaked in and out from behind towering maple trees—strategically swiveling between meticulously trimmed shrubbery and time-honored rose bushes, all the time looking over her shoulder to assure the FBI weren't following behind. Jinx spread out a blanket and unpacked the basket.

"I have some sandwiches with *lekvar*." She was hoping to impress them by using some of the new Hungarian words she'd been learning. *Lekvar*, she thought she remembered, meant jam.

"*Lekvár*," Aliz corrected her pronunciation.

They had just plopped down on the ground and unwrapped the wax paper-covered sandwiches when a big buxom girl with a shock of honey-colored hair and sky-blue eyes swooped in from nowhere. "What are you doing?" she asked.

Jinx startled. She had been praying they wouldn't get caught out beyond the established boundaries.

"Nothin' much. We're just havin' a little picnic."

"Really?" The curvaceous teenager pointed toward Albert. "What's your name?"

Albert gulped. His face turned beet red. He started stuttering, trying to spit out a response.

The intruder snickered at Albert. "Haven't you ever spoken to a girl before?"

The flush crept down Albert's neck and he turned his face away, seemingly embarrassed.

Jinx didn't appreciate the teenager causing Albert to feel uncomfortable. *Does she know he doesn't speak English very well? Is she trying to humiliate him? That ain't very neighborly.* "Are ya supposed to be out here?" Jinx's brow rose suspiciously, like her mama's always did when she doubted the validity of one of Jinx's wild stories.

"Well, uh. Not really."

"We got special permission to come out here for our picnic. So I would suggest that if you ain't got authorization to be out here, ya best mosey along."

The curvy shaped girl rudely stuck out her tongue at Jinx and walked away. Aliz stood up and started strutting around like a chicken. "Did you see the way she was walking?"

"She was flirting with Albert," Marianna added.

"Was not!" Albert blurted out—his face turning a deeper shade of crimson. Even his ears were as red as a ripe cherry.

Jinx tried not to laugh but he was a sight to see. Aliz started it first, just a giggle, then Benci. Then Marianna who couldn't control herself a minute longer, spit her strawberry jam sandwich all over poor Albert, who was sitting across from her. Albert joined in and pretty soon they rolled around on the ground laughing so hard they nearly killed themselves. Aliz peed her pants, which caused everyone to laugh even harder.

A moment later, two FBI agents appeared from behind the big oak tree. "Jinx!" They heard one of the big men shout, "Is that you?"

"We've done been caught. Run for it!" Jinx bellowed. The group of five sprinted toward the kitchen door at breakneck speed as the FBI followed at their heels. Holding onto her new fedora with one hand, she slung open the back door, pointed toward the pantry, where they disappeared into the low cabinet doors.

They could overhear the FBI agents informing Sibert, in a loud voice, the details about what had just taken place. It sounded as if they were standing right beside the pantry doors where the group had found a sanctuary of refuge. "Those kids aren't supposed to be out there, and Jinx knows this."

"I'll have another talk with her," Sibert assured them.

The FBI agent moved closer to the pantry door. "Make sure you let her know the next time we see those children outside of the designated boundaries we are going to ship them off to a labor camp for children, where they'll be picking green beans out in a hot field all day long and the only thing they'll have to eat is carrots." If you want to know the truth of it, they all held their breaths—afraid to even make the slightest chirp.

Green beans and carrots? Jinx gulped. Her shoulders slumped down because she knew, for sure, that a good old scolding was coming her way. She waited for several long moments before whispering to her friends, "I think it's safe. Let's get out of here." She cracked open the door, and when she thought the coast was clear she signaled to Aliz, Benci, Albert, and Marianna. "Let's make a run for it."

They crawled out from doors of the pantry, then as soon as she quietly shut the door Sibert appeared from nowhere. "The FBI agents were just here and they were looking for five children who had ventured outside of the designated area. Was the FBI looking for you?"

"FBI agents?" Jinx asked in faux confusion. She leisurely scrutinized the ceiling and finally offered up, "I can't quite recall."

"You can't quite recall if the FBI was looking for you?" Sibert cringed. He ran his fingers through his hair. "Geez."

"Let me do the talkin'," she advised her friends.

They numbly nodded.

"Well… " she bit at her lip as she desperately tried to devise a believable story, "there may have been five *different* children out there havin' a picnic." She nodded. "Yep, they probably just looked like us."

"A case of mistaken identity?" Sibert let out a chuckle in spite of himself. "Get out of here and keep your nose clean."

Jinx swiped her nose with her shirtsleeve. "Do I have jam on my nose?"

"I meant to stay out of trouble." He pointed toward the door. "Go!"

Jinx muted her laugh. She loved the way Sibert's cheeks deepened to slashes when his mouth curved up at the corners. "Alrighty." She gestured to her friends. "Let's go to the pool."

For some reason, her mama never discussed the incident with her, most likely due to the news that arrived later in the day. Her friends would be leaving the beloved Greenbrier—very soon.

On the first of April, the Hungarians were transferred to the Grove Park Inn, in Asheville, North Carolina. The relocation had nothing to do with the off-grounds picnic Jinx had arranged, but she felt like it did. They moved out with their families to make room for nearly four hundred Japanese diplomats who had been living at The Homestead, in Hot Springs, Virginia since December, and Jinx was heartbroken.

By mid-May she had made new companions and would often join them in the dining room where the Japanese would sit at the opposite side of the room from the Germans. One evening, while Jinx, Hinata, and Aiko were making rivers out of their mashed potatoes and gravy, the Germans started heckling the Japanese group when news arrived that Jimmy Doolittle had raided Tokyo. Jinx didn't care for them making fun of her friends, and she sure didn't like the way they were making light of the war. Her friend, Sammy, was over there fighting, and every night before she crawled into bed she prayed he would make it home alive.

She squirmed in her seat.

She was aware that all Japanese diplomats had had their assets frozen by the United States Government, because she had overheard Sibert telling her mama the news. However, for some reason unbeknownst to Jinx, the Germans were allowed to keep their money. She also knew the German diplomats had bought everything in the gift shop that hadn't been bolted down.

She felt ashamed when she noticed tears well up in the eyes of Hinata and Aiko's mother. After all, their mama hadn't started the war.

She didn't understand all this political stuff, but the longer she listened to them the angrier she got. Jinx was as hot as a firecracker lit at both ends by the time she leapt up onto the seat of her chair and started hollering at the Germans seated on the other side of the room. Every derogatory slam she could remember started rolling off her tongue, just like a sinner on a Saturday night.

"Ya'll spend money faster than green grass goin' through a goose, but they ain't got their money 'cause the government took it all."

"Shut up, kid." She heard a man shout back. She glared at him. They made eye contact and Jinx noted his sneering smile was like oil sliding over glass.

"You're 'bout as welcome here as a skunk at a church picnic." Jinx kept eggin' him on.

Stillness filled the room. Even the sound of silverware clanking against china dishes came to a complete halt.

She pointed toward the large man and secured her stance on the chair. "I wouldn't pee on ya if ya was on fire." Her eyes darted from one distorted face to another before settling on the mean man.

A slow flush crept up the man's neck. He stood up, but the lady next to him put her hand on his arm, and he lowered back down into his seat.

Unfortunately, Sibert was walking by the dining room at the time and witnessed Jinx's outburst. He walked over to her, asked her calmly to step down from the chair and escorted her to the kitchen. Her mama's eyes grew as wide as saucers as she listened to the words that had escaped her daughter's mouth. Her lips were fixed into the taut, pained shape they always assumed when she disapproved of her daughter's actions, then her face twisted into a shape Jinx had never seen before. The moment her mama clutched the wooden spoon Sibert and Roberto quickly found an excuse to leave.

"Well, I need to rush off and tend to some… some… chores."

"I'll help you." Roberto chimed in.

They scampered out of the kitchen leaving a mere child alone with an angry woman who had just snatched up a very large wooden spoon. Jinx knew she'd soon be a rotting carcass—just like a dead possum on the side of the road.

The first swat stung her leg. "Why in the tarnation were you using barn language in the dining room?"

Jinx screamed at the top of her lungs. "Don't beat me, Mama!"

The second wallop was followed by, "This is for being disrespectful!"

Jinx bellowed like a banshee rooster. Her anguished cries could be heard resonating down the hallway.

"I'm not even hittin' you hard, Jinx." Her mama whacked her again. "Stop it!"

"You're killin' me, Mama!" she wailed dramatically.

"And this one is for standing on the furniture."

Smack!

"Ouch!" Jinx rubbed her buttocks. "I ain't ever got scolded for standing on the furniture before. That ain't fair, Mama."

The last thwack barely grazed her. "This one is for actin' like your papa."

"For actin' like Papa? Mama, we've got to stand up for other folks. Just like Papa did." Tears filled Jinx's huge green eyes. "I miss him, too."

Her mama's gaze lowered and she vacantly stared at the floor for a long moment. Jinx noticed a hint of sadness stealing across her face. Her lips started trembling, and she turned to hug her daughter. They stood for a long spell, clutching one another tightly, hot tears running down their cheeks.

Jinx could hear the door crack open and rapidly close again.

"I'm sorry, Mama. I don't want ya to be ashamed of me."

Her mama just held her tighter.

Jinx stayed awake that night, lying in her bed, staring at the ceiling. Thoughts just kept rolling through her head; *forgiveness, forgiveness, revenge, forgiveness, revenge, revenge.* She started plotting and speculating on how she could settle the score with those loudmouthed Germans. Her mama had taught her about forgiveness and she knew it would be the better route to go, but she just didn't think she was ready to forgive them. The perfect plan suddenly formulated in the eleven-year-old's mind. She knew what she needed to do.

Perfect.

The following morning, just as Roberto was perching the jumbo lump crab on the hash, she volunteered to help roll the dishes into the dining room. She strategically placed a raw 'Scorned Woman' pepper underneath each lump of crab, which was to be served to the Germans who had caused Hinata and Aiko's mama to cry.

She knew most folks had never even heard of the 'Scorned Woman' pepper, let alone tasted one. However, she had sampled one, just a nibble a few weeks back when Rosie Shuler brought some up from her farm, and it was as hot as blue blazes. Rosie had said they were the hottest peppers east of the Alamo. They were so spicy, in fact, that Roberto had put them away to use at a later date. He figured if they dried out a while they might be able to use some minuscule slices in a few months, or perhaps crush them up to use as a spice eventually.

Jinx tilted her fedora to one side, crossed her arms, leaned back against the doorframe and watched with delight as the faces of the folks seated at table thirteen began contorting. Glasses of water were slammed down throats. They started gagging and coughing uncontrollably, the tears cascading down their cheeks. One man stood up, causing his chair to crash to the ground. He clutched his throat. His ugly pale face turned scarlet.

Jinx winked at Hinata and Aiko who were chortling energetically on the other side of the room. Even their mama had a wide smile on her face.

"Jinx!" She heard Sibert call out.

She ducked into a nearby doorway for a second and then casually reappeared. She cupped her hand around his arm. "Did ya know those Germans have been missing the dart board in the Virginia Room?" Her brow rose as she examined his face. "There are holes in all the murals Mr. Grauer painted."

Sibert's face turned bright red with anger. "They are extremely disrespectful."

Did I just see a puff of steam rising from his ears? Jinx imagined.

Sibert kept huffing. "Do you know what just happened in the dining hall?"

"Well," she paused momentarily, "someone *may* have placed a raw 'Scorned Woman' pepper underneath each lump of crab in the hash."

"Rosie Shuler's peppers?"

"Yep."

"So, do you know who did it?"

Jinx didn't respond.

He gave her a wink. "If you ever find out who is responsible, please give them a pat on the back for me."

Jinx paused, as if she was considering the timeline of events, and continued with her story. "Six weeks later the Greenbrier Resort's peculiar two hundred and one days of emergency government service came to an end. The bellman, maids, waiters and porters counted it all up and figured they had made over sixty-five thousand dollars in gratuities by the time all the folks had caught the train heading to New York."

"Wow! The diplomats were very generous."

"The diplomats were openhanded, for sure."

"So, was it business as usual after they left?"

"For six short weeks, the Greenbrier reopened its doors to regular guests. However, before the last foreign diplomat was exchanged, representatives of the United State Military contacted the manager, again. The Army wanted to use the resort as a hospital." Jinx pulled a yellowed newspaper clipping out and read it aloud.

"On and after September 1, 1942, the Greenbrier and cottages and its surrounding estate will be closed, in preparation for government use and, therefore, no further business can be accepted after that date.
This marks the end of the chapter of the Greenbrier's service to the public "Since 1778" as America's Most Beautiful Resort and the beginning of another chapter of service to our country."

"I had no idea the government could just... just take over a building."

"The Greenbrier was condemned under the War Powers Act and the government paid the Chesapeake and Ohio Railroad a little over three million dollars for the resort's facilities and land. Then, there was a quick attempt to sell the entire contents, but apparently no one needed six hundred rooms of furniture, so it was sold, donated, and pieced out to museums, universities, orphanages, schools, and hospitals. The staff was in a frantic rush to move out and most of the china, silver, prints, mirrors and miscellaneous items were auctioned off at the White Sulphur Springs railroad station."

"Then they just transformed it into a hospital?" This seemed like a lofty undertaking, considering all the equipment that would be needed to operate a hospital.

"They turned the fifth and sixth floors into a surgical unit and added a massive elevator to the front of the hotel so they could transport patients and equipment up to the operating rooms. The historical cottages were the living quarters of the doctors and nurses who came here to work, and what is now the Presidential Suite was used as a maternity ward."

"Why would they need a maternity ward?"

"Sometimes wives would come to visit their husbands and would go into labor."

"They thought of everything, eh?"

"They considered every minute detail. The main lobby wasn't altered very much. It was, as always, stylish and sophisticated, but there was a chapel added, and the ballroom became the recreation area packed full with Ping-Pong tables, chess sets, and other games to help pass the time."

"Were you allowed to use the recreation area?"

"I had full access to the recreation area, and that was where I learned to play checkers."

"What else do you remember?"

"They used the Mineral Bath Department for physical therapy for the recuperating soldiers, and of course, all the soldiers had access to the golf courses, tennis courts, and indoor swimming pool."

"Did everyone continue to work here?

"Most folks stayed on, including Sibert and my mama. But Roberto, the chef, wasn't offered a position because they weren't convinced he could acclimate to the change of Army cuisine." Jinx started laughing like it was the silliest thing she had ever heard. "Fortunately, Freddie and Ms. Alice kept their jobs. But the Army used free labor by putting the prisoners of war to work."

"They housed prisoners of war here?"

"It was a very extravagant prison camp."

"I would say so."

"During war time, I mostly followed on the heels of the nurses. I firmly believe that being part of the Ashford General Hospital made me who I am today." Her eyes popped open as if something important had just occurred to her. "I wouldn't have earned a medical degree had I not experienced caring for those soldiers." A reminiscent grin suddenly wrapped up around her cheeks. "I haven't told you about Doctor Burl yet, have I?"

Dr. Burl

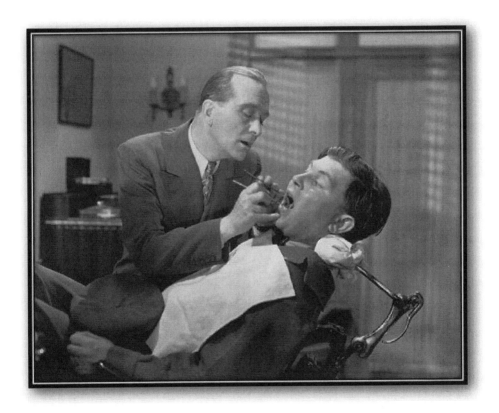

Dr. Burl
September 1942

JINX DROPPED DOWN into the waiting room chair, unwrapped a strawberry jam sandwich and looked around at the soldiers who were seated beside her. The young man to her right flashed a smile and she could see he was missing several teeth.

"Would ya like a piece of my sandwich?" she offered, "I could pinch ya off a portion."

"No," he replied appreciatively, "thanks for offering."

Jinx couldn't understand how anyone would pass up the opportunity to taste the best strawberry jam in the state of West Virginia, so she just shrugged her shoulders. "Alrighty then."

"Jinx," she heard the receptionist call her name, "Dr. Burl can see you now."

She wrapped the remainder of her sandwich up and tucked it into the new purse her mama had stitched up for her. She followed the receptionist down a long hallway and into a door where she saw a dental chair, which had two encyclopedias, apparently being used as a booster, stacked on the seat. Even though Jinx was twelve years old, her petite body structure would lead one to believe she was much younger. She didn't figure she needed the encyclopedias as a booster, but when she examined the large seat she determined otherwise.

"Hello, Jinx. I'm Dr. Burl."

"Hi, Dr. Burl. It's a pleasure to meet ya."

"Likewise." He studied her curiously. "I didn't see an appointment scheduled for you today. Do you have an emergency? Is something specific bothering you?"

"Nope." Jinx proceeded to climb up into the chair and plopped down on top of the encyclopedias. "My mama suggested I come to see ya just to have ya check me out." She opened her mouth wide.

The doctor chose a long metal object with a mirror attached at one end and looked around inside her mouth. "Did you brush your teeth today?"

"Of course I scrubbed my teeth today. My mama would beat me to death with a wooden spoon if I didn't scrub my teeth in the morning."

Dr. Burl looked at her doubtfully. "Is that so?" He placed the long handled mirror back onto the tray. "I met your mama, and she doesn't seem like the type of woman who would beat her child to death with a wooden spoon."

Jinx's eyes grew wide. "Ya know my mama?" She swallowed deeply, fidgeted in her seat and hem-hawed around. "Okay, Dr. Burl, I might as well tell ya the truth. My mama didn't send me. So don't tell her I stopped in. Okay?"

"I won't mention a word," he promised, before sheepishly inserting, "your mama is a very beautiful woman."

"Yep. She's smart, too."

Dr. Burl blurted out, "Do you have a daddy?"

Jinx scrunched up her nose. "That's a silly question, Dr. Burl. Of course I have a papa. He's in heaven now 'cause he died in a coal mining accident."

"I'm sorry."

"Thank ya." Jinx responded. "It was a few years back."

"Did your mama remarry?"

"Nope." She shook her head. "She ain't divorced."

Dr. Burl chuckled and picked up a curvy metal tool. "Open wide again, please." He probed around. "Have you been eating strawberry jam?"

"Well, I'll be! That's amazin'." She punched him lightly on the shoulder. "How'd ya know I was eatin' jam? Ya must be a really good doctor."

"There appears to be a couple hundred strawberry seeds wedged in your teeth. Otherwise, your teeth look very healthy." He placed the utensil back on the tray. "So, Jinx. What is the reason for your visit today?"

She inhaled deeply before divulging her plan. "I was hopin' ya'd be able to make me some false teeth."

"Jinx, your teeth are beautiful and healthy. Why do you want false teeth?"

She started pointing to various teeth as she explained. "I want a pair I can slip into my mouth over the top of my other teeth. I'd like to have them look all crooked, and have them stickin' out in all directions, and maybe even have one of them black so it looks like I'm missing a front tooth."

His brows arched questioning. "Why?"

"So I can fool the soldiers when I make the rounds with Nurse Ella. It would make 'em laugh. Plus, I could tell 'em Dr. Burl fixed my teeth." She started cackling.

Dr. Burl joined along, unable to contain his laughter. "So, that is why they call you Jinx, huh?"

"Yep." She nodded. "What do ya say? Will ya do it for me?"

"I might be able to arrange something," he paused momentarily, "if you will give me permission to ask your mama to accompany me to dinner."

"Sure," Jinx shrugged, "but she's awful busy chasin' after me."

"I have no doubt," he mumbled. "Is it a deal?"

"It's a deal." Her big eyes looked up at him. "Do ya wanna shake on it?"

"Sure," he offered his hand.

Jinx's entire body started shaking and vibrating in the chair. Eventually, Dr. Burl caught on and started jerking and juddering along with her.

"Excuse me," they heard the receptionist say as she opened the door, "is everything all right in here?"

Dr. Burl flushed with embarrassment.

"We were just shakin' to seal our deal," Jinx explained.

"Okay…" the receptionist flashed a bright smile in Jinx's direction, "your next patient is in room two, Dr. Burl."

"Thank you," he replied. "I'll be there in a few moments."

They started giggling as soon as the door slapped shut.

Finally, Jinx sputtered out, "Ya can't tell my mama until after I have 'em. I wanna surprise her."

"That's fine, let me get some wax to take an imprint. Then I will need to play around with some Vulcanite rubber." He murmured underneath his breath, "it will take me a week or two."

"Thank ya, Dr. Burl. I appreciate it."

"I'll be right back."

"Okey, dokey," she said, as she pulled the remains of her sandwich from her purse and waited for him to return with the wax mold.

"Did the teeth turn out as you had hoped?"

"Dr. Burl did a wonderful job of creating me a pair of dentures. He made a mouthpiece that held six teeth. They were different shades of grungy yellow, he blackened out one of the front teeth, and made the rest of them poke out in multiple directions." Jinx grinned. "I kept them with me all the time and would stick them in my mouth when I wanted to make someone laugh. Although, my mama didn't laugh the first time I showed her. She nearly passed out cold on the floor when I told her Dr. Burl had fixed my teeth and I showed her my new smile."

I started laughing along just thinking about her mama's reaction.

"Then I borrowed a *Movie Stars Parade* magazine from Susan's workstation," she fessed up, "although Susan didn't know I had taken it. But anyway, the cover of the magazine had a beautiful picture of Veronica Lake on the front and I would hold it up over my mouth and walk around and ask the soldiers if they thought I looked like Veronica Lake. I would lower the magazine, flash them a big crooked smile and they would just hoot and holler around." Jinx beamed at the long lost memory.

"You were a rotten child," I told her.

"I was rambunctious."

"Did Dr. Burl ask your mama for a date?"

"Dr. Burl eventually asked for my mama's hand in marriage. They were married on Christmas Day of 1942. It was a small ceremony held in the chapel at the Greenbrier. Mama was steaming hot when she saw the photographs later, because I was wearing my false teeth in every one of pictures. Dr. Burl just laughed. He was a wonderful man and so gentle and kind. I loved him as much as Mama did and he was a very good father to me."

"It sounds like you were blessed."

"Do you know what, Dee? I have been blessed every single day of my life. When I consider where I could have ended up—staying in the filthy coal camp, compared to where I essentially grew up—here at the fabulous Greenbrier Hotel, well, there is no way to adequately express my gratitude." She confided, "I thank God every day for my multitude of blessings."

One early morning in May of 1943, Jinx woke smelling the sweet scent of frying bacon floating up the stairs and into her bedroom. She slid a sweater on over her pajamas, descended the narrow the staircase, and into the kitchen where she saw her mama whisking eggs. She caught the tantalizing scent of morning bread baking, and smiled, like she always did, when she saw the window crammed with pots of pungent geraniums.

"Good morning, Jinx. Could you run out and see if everything's going okay in the barn? I think Daisy Mae is still having her calf. She's been having contractions for hours."

"Yes, Mama." Jinx opened the screen door, stepped out onto the large wraparound porch, and tugged on her boots. She sleepily walked across the meadow toward the barn. When she shoved open the side door she could see Daisy Mae lying quite still, moaning on the barn floor. Dr. Burl was situated on the ground attempting to pull a calf from its mother's womb.

"Mama told me to come out and check on ya. Is everything okay?"

"The calf's head is stuck and there is no room to turn him around."

"Is it bad?"

"Yes, it is."

"Can I help ya?"

He withdrew his arm and located a rope, tied a slipknot on one end, and dropped to the barn floor again. "I'm going to have to push this thin, looped rope towards the calf's lower jaw with my fingers."

Dr. Burl's face lay down on the straw-covered barn floor in a puddle of filthy muck with his arm deep inside the straining cow. She heard him gag. "There's shit all over this floor."

Jinx could tell Dr. Burl was getting aggravated and pictured, in her mind, her mama chasing him around the kitchen with her big ole wooden spoon. She figured she'd better warn him. "I won't tell Mama ya were using barn language, 'cause the last time I used barn language she 'bout beat me to death with a wooden spoon."

Jinx could see the doubtful look on his face. "You can use barn language in the barn, Jinx," Dr. Burl said as his arm stretched in further and jolted when the little calf's tongue gave him a lick. "Just felt the little fellow's tongue."

"Let me ask ya this, Dr. Burl. Is that why they call it barn language? 'Cause ya can use it in the barn?"

"Yep."

"Can ya say pee in the barn?"

"Yep."

Jinx thought this all through carefully. "Well, shit. I didn't know that."

Dr. Burl let out a long sigh of resignation, braced himself, and plunged his arm in deep, with everything he had. He felt the noose slide over the sharp little incisor teeth and into the calf's lower jaw. "Jinx, come here and hold onto this rope. Hold it tight and pull when I tell you to."

Dr. Burl and Jinx grunted and pulled. Daisy Mae groaned and pushed. They rested a spell and pulled and pushed again.

"I'm concerned the calf may asphyxiate if we don't get him out of there soon."

"What does asphyxiate mean?" Jinx inquired.

"It means to smother. He isn't getting enough air."

Jinx nervously started chattering. "I almost asphyxiated one time. Yep, it was at my sixth birthday party and when I blew out my candles I nearly used up all my air."

Dr. Burl didn't respond.

"There was a whole bunch of candles on the cake." She let out a hot breath. "Everybody was scared to death. They thought I was a goner. It was a close call."

"I bet it was, Jinx. Now, pull!"

On their fourth attempt the head finally popped into view, and with one strenuous yank on Dr. Burl's part, the calf slid out. The calf lay motionless on the straw-covered floor and appeared to be dead. Dr. Burl quickly cleared the mucus from the calf's mouth and pressed on his ribs. The little fellow wheezed and his back legs jerked. Dr. Burl picked him up and laid him beside of his mother. "There you go, Daisy Mae. You did a fine job."

Jinx watched in awe as Daisy Mae begin to sniff and started probing at her calf. Soon, she was systematically licking him. A couple of minutes later the calf started trying to sit up. His head was shaking and he stumbled on the first try. Daisy Mae gave him a boost with her nose and he was standing on four legs.

"Did ya learn how to do this when ya were in school studying to become a dentist?"

"No," he pulled out a white handkerchief and wiped the filth from his face, "I grew up on a farm."

Jinx noisily exhaled. "Just watchin' Daisy Mae givin' birth to her calf made me dog-tired."

"Me too," Dr. Burl admitted as the sweat poured down his brow.

"Dr. Burl," Jinx gravely informed him, "it's a good thing your patients didn't see what ya just did 'cause they sure enough wouldn't want ya stickin' your fingers in their mouth anymore."

He examined his bloody and secretion stained hands. "That's for sure."

"Can I draw ya a hot bath?"

"Thanks, Jinx. I'd appreciate it."

The following day, Jinx bounced into the hotel and immediately located Ms. Alice, the maid, who would often give her treasures from the lost and found closet.

"How are ya doin', Ms. Alice?"

"I'm doin' just fine, Jinx. How are you? Have you been practicing those dance steps I taught you last week?"

"I sure have. Let me show ya." Jinx stepped back with her right foot, met her right foot with her left, went back on her left foot and twirled in a circle. Boom! She hit the floor. Quickly hopping back up, she explained, "I ain't quite got the turn part yet, but I'll keep workin' on it."

Ms. Alice was always unfailingly cheerful. "You're doing just fine. Keep practicing. You're going to need to know how to twirl gracefully when you start dancing with the boys."

"I will." Jinx brushed the rear of her trousers off. "Have ya seen Nurse Ella? I wanna tell her something."

"Not today. Try the infirmary."

Jinx scampered off and peeked in various rooms. Finally, she spotted Nurse Ella and approached her from behind. "Have ya been gettin' into any trouble, Nurse Ella?"

The big boned woman with long brown hair glanced over her shoulder. "I should be the one asking you that question, Jinx."

"Nope. I ain't caused no trouble today." Jinx shook her head convincingly then started chattering like a magpie. "Ya ain't gonna believe what happened yesterday. Dr. Burl had his arm, all the way up to his shoulder, in Daisy Mae's rear end."

"Who is Daisy Mae?"

"Our cow."

"Okay. Good," she paused. "I think."

"He was rollin' around in chicken and cow poop, there's another word for poop but ya can only use it when you're in the barn. But anyway, he pushed his arm all the way up… "

Nurse Ella held her hand up in an attempt to stop Jinx from talking. "I don't want to know this Jinx. Dr. Burl is my dentist and I don't want to visualize where his hands have been."

"That's what I said, too. Anyway, he fetched a rope and shoved his arm… "

"Stop." Nurse Ella turned and was about to hand Jinx a clipboard, but she noticed a bloodstain on Jinx's britches. Her gaze rose and for the first time she realized Jinx was beginning to develop breasts. "Oh, dear." She rushed to a nearby table, found a white apron and instructed the little girl to wrap it around her waist. "Jinx, I hate to tell you this but I believe you are bleeding."

"Bleeding?" She started examining her knees. "Where? Do I need to get some stitches? I'm scuffin' my knees up all the time when I'm climbin' the oak tree out front."

"No, honey. I didn't mean to alarm you. I think you have started your menstrual cycle," she quietly said as the girl tied the apron at her waist. "We should go find your mama and have… we should have… the woman talk."

"The woman talk?" Jinx questioned.

"Yes, sorry." The nurse opened a high cabinet door and removed a brown paper poke before they scampered down the long corridor and to the wing where Nurse Ella knew Jinx's mama would be working in the kitchen.

Nurse Ella whispered something into her mama's ear.

"Oh." Her mama startled. "She's not even thirteen years old yet."

"I know, but you can never tell when it's going to start." She handed her the paper bag.

Jinx's mama shuffled her into the bathroom, removed the contents of the paper bag, and showed Jinx how to attached a Kotex disposable pad to a reusable sanitary belt. "I'll be right back." She returned in a couple of moments carrying a clean pair of britches for the little girl to slide on.

They promptly returned to the kitchen where her mama and Nurse Ella attempted to clarify the particulars of what had just occurred—well, kind of.

"Jinx," her mama said, "you are a young woman now and what happened today is a very natural thing. All girls, at around your age, start their menstrual cycle. It is perfectly normal and nothing to be embarrassed over. Right, Nurse Ella?"

"Yes," she nodded in assurance, "this happens to all girls when they start growing up."

"Only girls?" Jinx thought this through. "Ya mean the boys don't have to go through this?"

"No, only girls."

"Well, that ain't fair."

"I agree." Nurse Ella thoughtfully responded. "I know the bleeding is a bit of a shock the first time but you should not be concerned."

"So true." Her mama agreed.

"Mama," her eyes narrowed, "ya could have told me 'bout this earlier! Were ya just waitin' for me to be surprised?"

"I did tell you."

Jinx's face scrunched up. "Ya did not."

"Do you remember when I was describing how the kittens came into this world?"

"Yeah."

"Then there was the story explaining how you don't need to buy a cow if you can get the milk for free."

"Huh?"

"I told you why Jack Woodward's dog keeps havin' puppies."

"I'm still not understanding what Jack's dog or a cow's milk has to do with any of this."

"It's not exactly like Jack's dog."

"Okay, but it is like Daisy Mae, right?"

"Kinda."

"So, ya really *didn't* explain it to me."

"Well… you see, Jinx, married folks do the same thing."

"Oh." Jinx cringed, disturbing visions started flashing through her mind. "You and Dr. Burl do it?"

Her mama's cheeks reddened. "Yes, we do."

"Just like Jack Woodward's dog?"

"Kinda."

"Oh Lordy, Mama. That is disgusting!" She gagged. "I ain't ever gonna get married."

The women exchanged knowing glances.

Jinx sighed. "How many times is this gonna happen?"

"Every month," Nurse Ella replied. "Maybe not every month at first, but eventually you will have a menstrual cycle every month at around the same time."

"Every month? This is horrible! I am mortified!" Her forehead dropped down to the table. Her right hand started pounding over and over again against the tabletop. "Mortified!" She peeked up for a second. "I just learned that word this week. Mortified was on my vocabulary list at school." She lowered her head again and moaned melodramatically.

Nurse Ella's attention turned to her mama. "I also heard Maidenform Brassier Company has started selling training bras so it may be a good idea to purchase one for Jinx since her breasts are beginning to develop."

Jinx's mama slowly nodded.

"A training bra? For my breasts?" Jinx screeched. "What will I be training 'em for?"

The two grownups stared at each other for a long drawn out moment. They both shrugged their shoulders. Finally, her mama confessed, "I'm not sure what training bras are meant to train, but I do know if you have menstrual cramps I can brew up a cup of ginger tea."

"Cramps?" the preteen huffed. "Ya'll ain't being much help here."

"I have a book you can read, Jinx." Nurse Ella recommended. "It explains everything and has a few drawings to help you understand what is happening."

"I already read your book." Jinx rolled her eyes. "I snatched it off your bookshelf a few weeks back and learned all 'bout puberty and sexual reproduction." She hopped down from her chair, walked over to the lower pantry, where she stored her precious belongings, dug through a pile of books, found the one she was searching for, and slammed *Puberty Explained* on the table.

"You took my book?" A frown formed on the nurse's face.

"I *borrowed* your book. I was gonna return it."

Jinx's mama squinted before pointing at the medical textbook. "Can I see it?"

Jinx slid it across the table. "How 'bout I fix us all a cuppa tea and if ya'll think of anything else I need to know, now might be a fine time to share—since we're havin' the woman talk, and all."

Her mama addressed Nurse Ella. "Why is this harder on me than her?"

Nurse Ella released a sympathetic sigh followed by a nod of her head. "I can only empathize with you."

Her mama skimmed through the illustrated pages. "Jinx, could you add a pinch of Chamomile to my tea? I need to calm down. Please grab us a few cookies, too."

Nurse Ella added. "Could you add a splash of brandy to mine, please?"

"So," I summarized, "your first lesson regarding sexual education included helping Daisy Mae give birth, having your mama explain why your neighbor's dog kept having puppies, and reading an illustrated textbook?"

"That is how I learned about the birds and the bees."

"I always think it is interesting to hear how people first learn about puberty. It seems everyone has a different tale and most can remember the exact day with absolute clarity."

"Truthfully, my mama was a little vague on the details, but I consider myself lucky she even broached the topic at all. They didn't teach sex education in school back then and many parents didn't feel comfortable enough to have *the talk* with their children. So, all in all, I would say I was fairly well-prepared for the shocking news."

"I still recall the day I first had my period, too. I was fortunate to have had a mother who explained what to expect."

"It is a parent's job." Jinx thoughtfully added, "Although, in today's world, I would expect most children have been exposed to the topic through television and the Internet, well before they reach the age when they should know these things."

"I totally agree."

We sat in comfortable silence for a few moments before Jinx blurted out, "Let me tell you about meeting the duchess."

"The duchess?"

Cookies with the Duchess

Cookies with the Duchess
October 1943

JINX STOOD OUTSIDE the kitchen door. Her oversized sweater was protecting her from the crisp fall weather that had settled into the Allegheny Mountains of West Virginia, prematurely this season. She consciously observed the breathtaking views of rolling hills, flanked with soaring pine, maple, and oak trees. The newly changing hues of orange and golden leaves were just starting to peek out. Her attention shifted toward the line of automobiles inching their way up the long driveway leading to the front entrance. She shoved open the side door and saw her mama filling a large teapot with water. "This place has been open for a year, Mama. I don't understand why they're having the dedication after all this time."

"You should know how the government works by now, Jinx. Besides, it's going to be an exciting day around here. The Duke and Duchess of Windsor are touring the new facility and will be signing autographs for the patients. There's going to be a ton of guests here today. Folks from all over the place are coming to see how the Greenbrier Hotel was transformed into Ashford General Hospital." She turned and shook her finger at her daughter. "Be on your best behavior today. I mean it. No false teeth!"

"Yes, ma'am." Jinx figured this was the ideal time to have a chat with the Duchess of Windsor, seeing how she had never met a real duchess before. It would be a perfect day to ask her to sign her special book, so she followed behind the duchess, at about a pace of twenty feet, all day long. Finally, a man dressed in an important military uniform, with dozens of badges sewn on his jacket, approached the duke and asked if he could speak with him in private. She watched the two men go into a room and shut the door.

Jinx took her chance. She casually strolled over to where the duchess was seated. Her dark hair was glistening, seemingly melding with the black silk dress she was donning. Jinx admired the bright red lipstick that made her lips appear large and plump and the diamond and ruby brooch pinned on her collar.

"Are ya the Duchess of Windsor?

"Yes, but please call me Wallis."

"Hi, Wallis. It's a pleasure to meet ya. My name is Jinx."

"Really? I have a dear friend named Jinx Falkenberg.

"Ya know somebody else named Jinx?"

"I do. She is a very beautiful and famous model."

"Well, I'll be." The little girl sat down, unwrapped two peanut butter cookies, which she had swiped from the kitchen, and offered one to the duchess. "Would ya like a cookie? They're peanut butter and mighty tasty."

"Maybe just a nibble." Wallis confessed, "I'm trying to maintain my figure. A woman can't be too rich or too thin."

"I don't know 'bout that. Mrs. Woodward probably wishes she wasn't so thin." Jinx graciously handed a cookie and paper napkin to the woman.

"Thank you." The duchess glanced down at the splintered cookie, which the little girl had been carrying around in her pocket all day. "Who is Mrs. Woodward?"

"Mrs. Woodward is Jack's mama," Jinx exhaled noisily. "Everyone's been gossipin' 'bout her."

"Who is Jack?"

"Oh, he used to be my pesky neighbor who made stinker noises by puttin' his hand under his armpit. I still see him at school, but he ain't my neighbor anymore 'cause Mama married Dr. Burl and we moved into his farmhouse."

Wallis pinched a smidgen of her cookie off before reiterating, "Stinker noises with his hand under his armpit?" She popped the morsel into her mouth.

"Yep. He don't make stinker noises anymore. Now he just plays songs."

"What a... a... an amazing talent."

"Not really," Jinx assured. "I mean, he's fifteen years old and is still making armpit noises. Do boys ever grow up?"

"I'm not quite sure." Wallis shrugged her shoulders. "Do tell, what did Jack's mother do to prompt people to gossip about her?"

"Oh, she was hittin' the bottle pretty heavy over at the waterin' hole last Saturday night." Jinx looked at her frankly. "She was there without her husband," she added two exaggerated nods of her head to emphasize her point. "That woman sure can dance the tail off of a monkey. Anyway, the button on her skirt snapped off and her skirt fell down over her skinny, little hips and plopped, right smack-dab, down on the dance floor," Jinx started cackling, "and she wasn't wearin' any under panties."

Wallis' hand rose to cover her mouth. "Oh! How embarrassing."

"Yep. Ms. Alice, she's the maid here, said it was downright disgraceful." Jinx took a bite of her cookie as she glanced around the room. "Was it you and your husband who created quite a..." her eyes shot up to the ceiling, in an attempt to pull back the word she had overheard the woman in the beauty salon saying, "a shamble?"

"Scandal, I believe, is the word you are searching for," she replied candidly. "We did, I suppose one could say, create quite a scandal."

"Was it worth it?"

"Yes, it was."

"Alrighty then, how does a person go 'bout gettin' in a scandal? I was just wonderin' 'cause I might wanna be in one someday." Jinx considered this carefully, "Although, I don't wanna be like Jack's mama and wind up showin' my rear end to everybody at the waterin' hole."

"Good choice," Wallis confirmed, "one should always wear under panties."

"I think so too." Jinx nudged her new friend. "So, what'd ya'll do?"

"We'll let me see..." Wallis seemed to prudently deliberate on how much information to divulge to a thirteen-year-old girl. "I fell in love with King Edward the Eighth, and he fell in love with me. Unfortunately, at the time, I was married to someone else. The man I was married to, by the way, was not faithful. I filed for a divorce in order to marry King Edward."

"I know all 'bout divorce. I read the details in *Look* magazine. Is that how everybody found 'bout ya'll? Was it in *Look* magazine?"

"Oh, most certainly at some point or another. It was printed in various newspapers and magazines and this distressed his mother and his brother, who was the Duke of York. Some people felt the king should not marry a woman who had two living ex-husbands."

Jinx interrupted, "It wasn't your fault your ex-husbands were still livin'."

"Very true. Nonetheless, since he wanted to marry me, it caused a constitutional crisis in the United Kingdom and the Dominions. His relationship with me made him very unpopular with the conservative-led British government, mainly because the Church of England does not permit the remarriage of divorced people who have living ex-spouses. Ultimately, our marriage led to his abdication in December of 1936."

"What's an abdication?"

"A resignation, I suppose you could say."

"What happened then?"

"Edward's brother became king. His name was George and he created the title of Duke of Windsor for Edward."

"So, now you're the Duchess of Windsor."

"Yes, I am."

"Is the duke rich?"

"He is."

"So, ya'll fell in love and since ya were divorced folks started gossipin' 'bout ya?"

"Yes, some people say we created a scandal."

"That's all ya'll did?" Jinx's jaw dropped open in total disbelief. "Are ya kiddin' me? There are all kinda folks who visit the Greenbrier who are divorced." She reached over and patted the duchess' hand to console her. "I reckon ya had to be brave to get through it all."

"Fortunately, I have a fearless spirit."

"My mama says I'm fearless—just like my papa was."

"Good for you. One should always strive to be gallant."

"Yep." Jinx leaned over and whispered, "I won't let the cat out of the bag concernin' your scandal."

"Thank you, Jinx." Wallis stifled a laugh.

"Wallis," Jinx reached out and touched her silk dress, "you're dressed so sophisticated and ya talk nice, too. I was just wonderin' what do ya think 'bout this? My schoolteacher, her name is Mrs. Jones, keeps tellin' me that ain't ain't a word and ya ain't supposed to say it. Do ya agree with her?"

"I don't quite know." The beautiful woman seemed to ponder this astutely. "I ain't ever used the word ain't," she finally responded teasingly. "However, if I were you, I'd listen to your schoolteacher. Teachers are full of knowledge and wisdom."

"Okay." Jinx nodded. "Hey Wallis, would ya care to sign my book? Eleanor gave it to me on my sixth birthday."

"Are you kidding? I would love to autograph your book."

Jinx handed her the special pen and pointed out Eleanor's inscription on the front page.

"Very impressive."

"Yep. Eleanor is a friend of mine."

Wallis Warfield Simpson, the Duchess of Windsor, placed the embossed leather journal on the side table and conveyed the following wisdom:

> A woman can't be too rich or too thin.
> (But just in case ~ always wear your under panties)
> Wallis Warfield Simpson
> The Duchess of Windsor
> October '43

"I'm sure glad I met ya, Wallis. If ya ever come here with your friend, Jinx, will ya look me up? I'd love to meet another Jinx."

"I certainly will," the duchess guaranteed. "Thanks for the cookie."

"You're welcome. I hope ya have a good day."

"You too, little lady."

"So, did you ever get to meet the other Jinx?"

"I had the opportunity to meet Jinx Falkenburg on several occasions. The first time I met her was when she and the duchess were having tea. She was as excited as I was when the duchess introduced us and we both had an opportunity to meet someone else named Jinx. Since we shared the same name we had a common bond."

"I'm not really familiar with Jinx Falkenburg. Why was she so famous?"

"Jinx was absolutely gorgeous! She was an actress, a tennis star, and an accomplished swimmer, and one of the highest paid cover girl supermodels in the United States during the 1930's and 40's. She married a journalist who was named Tex McCrary and soon after the *Tex and Jinx* show hit the radio and they were stars in the early days of television."

"What type of show did they have? I've never seen it."

"The couple hosted a modern talk show where they interviewed celebrities and discussed important topics of the day."

"Did she sign your autograph book?"

The elderly woman smiled brightly. "Both Jinx and her husband autographed my book. She wrote, 'From one Jinx to another' and Tex, her husband, drew a little sketch of me in the book. It was the first time anyone ever drew a picture in the journal." She paused as if she could picture the scene in her mind. "Tex was a very handsome man and quite an accomplished artist. They were a striking couple." She tilted her head and winked at me. "I'm getting ahead of myself. I didn't meet Jinx and Tex until after the war, and I need to tell you the stories about when the Greenbrier was the Shangri-La for wounded soldiers."

Shangri-La for Wounded Soldiers

Shangri-La for Wounded Soldiers
November 1943

———— ❧ ————

WEARING A WHITE nurse's cap, Jinx made her rounds on the heels of Nurse Ella. Since her mama had strictly forbidden her to be anywhere in the hotel without a woman present in the room, she had spent several months following the nurses around, asking questions, and generally talking their leg off. Eventually, a group of them held a ceremony where they presented Jinx with her own white cap that had a special Red Cross pin fastened on the rim. Additionally, they bestowed her with the very prestigious title of Honorary Junior Nurse—a designation that she was mighty proud of.

In November of 1943, there was a young soldier admitted to the hospital. Dr. Elkin, who ran the neurosurgical center, had operated on him two days earlier and he still lay unconscious in the recovery area of the six-hundred-bed unit. The impassive expression on his face, the lack of color in his cheeks, and the sheer motionlessness of his body troubled Jinx.

"Is he ever gonna wake up, Nurse Ella?"

"I do hope so, Jinx."

"Is there anything I can do to help him?" she asked, as she stared at the bandages wrapped around his head. Her eyes flashed toward the maroon-colored robe hanging on a hook beside his cot. She had become familiar seeing the soldiers walking around the grounds, clad in maroon robes and pajama bottoms. It was a stark contrast to the furs and fine suits, which were usually sported in great fashion at the resort.

"Why don't you read to him? Or you can even talk to him. I believe he can hear us even though he isn't talking back. It might be good for him to have someone visit him every day. Your voice would become familiar to him and it might help him to wake up."

Jinx studied his chart and saw his name was Thomas. "Howdy, Thomas." She pulled up a fold-up chair and scooted it to his side. "My name is Jinx, and I have been assigned to your case. Don't ya worry 'bout nothin' 'cause I'm an Honorary Junior Nurse, so rest assured you're in good hands. Nurse Ella told me ya were sleeping and ya wouldn't be talkin' back to me much, and that's alright 'cause my mama says I can talk a blue streak, so I'm sure I can do enough talkin' for the both of us. I figured I could go over my geography lessons with ya every day, 'cause it's my worst subject in school. Then, if we ever start gettin' *Look* magazine in again, I'll read some of those articles to ya. *Look* magazine is my favorite. When the diplomats moved in, the only available newspaper was *The New York Times*. I reckon the government wanted to make sure they weren't readin' stuff they shouldn't be, so the good magazines disappeared right off the shelf and they haven't brought all of 'em back yet. Sibert told me we should be gettin' *Look* magazine back in soon though." She peeped at him. "I'm sure you're as happy 'bout that as I am."

Jinx pulled out a stack of *The New York Times,* chose the one on top, and rapidly scanned the articles.

Allies Go Ashore in Italy
American Bombers Attack in Great Force

"I figure ya don't wanna hear anymore news comin' from the frontlines of the war so I'll just read the good stuff to ya. Okay, Thomas?"

She smoothed the crease in the paper and laid it on the side of his bed. *This is a good one.* She tapped her finger on the specific article. "*Casablanca* is more fun than the real thing. You must remember this: Last spring, the American and British forces began a drive against the Germans in Morocco. Meanwhile, Humphrey Bogart and Ingrid Bergman shot a film called *Casablanca* on a Hollywood soundstage. The film is now in theaters. As time goes by, it may prove more memorable than the real thing. Bogey plays a nightclub owner who runs into an old flame at his Moroccan hideaway. He sacrifices his happiness for hers while serving the Allied underground. Dooley Wilson plays a fine piano player, and Claude Rains is an unflappable chief of police."

Jinx folded the newspaper up and tucked it under her arm. "I might be a movie star someday, Thomas. I haven't decided yet. I kinda figure I have a little bit of time before I need to make a firm decision." She sighed dramatically. "I've also been thinkin' 'bout gettin' myself into a scandal. Ya know, like the Duchess of Windsor, or Jack's mama. I haven't told ya that story yet, but folks are still talkin' 'bout what Jack's mama did down at the waterin' hole—not that I wanna get into a scandal like she did. Plus, I'm not supposed to be talkin' 'bout folks 'cause Eleanor once told me that 'small minds discuss people' and I don't want to have a small mind." Jinx shrugged her shoulders. "I don't know. I'm still thinkin' on it." She tenderly patted his hand. "I'll see ya tomorrow right after school."

The following day, Jinx rushed to Thomas' bedside immediately after she got in from school. "Hey, Thomas. It's me. Jinx. I'm visiting with ya again today and decided to bring ya some treats." She unwrapped a chocolate chip cookie and held it close to his nose. "Just smell this. Isn't it wonderful? I believe chocolate chip cookies smell better than anything else I can think of, don't you?" She pinched off a diminutive sliver of chocolate and placed the tiny morsel on his tongue. "If ya wake up I promise to bring ya a whole plate of cookies fresh out of the oven." She walked over to the table and carefully picked up the cup of tea her mama had brewed using the healing water and Holy Basil, which is used to combat stress. "My mama sometimes brews her specialty tea using the water from the Springhouse, usually if someone needs to cleanse their body." Jinx inserted a suction tube into the cup and withdrew a fraction of the liquid. "It also works for folks who have bumped their head." She parted his lips and squirted a minuscule drop onto his tongue. "Bottoms up."

She settled back into her chair and creased open the newspaper. "Let's see what we have today." She scanned the articles. "This one looks funny. It has a picture of a whole line of donkeys and they are wearing straw hats and they have on scarfs and beads hanging around their necks. The headline says,

'Bring Your Ass to Town Day'." She peered over the top of the newspaper. "Don't tell my mama I said that word. Okay, Thomas? Anyway, the article says everyone should come and start shopping for Christmas and if ya bring your donkey to town for the parade, the winner who has the best dressed donkey will receive a complimentary case of soda pop and free bales of hay from Miller's Seed and Feed. Wouldn't it be a fun parade to see? I think so. I wonder if ya don't have a donkey if ya could dress up your cat or your dog? I'm gonna ask my mama if she would drive me down to Tennessee for the parade. I doubt she will, but why not ask?" Jinx peeked at Thomas, stretched over and grasped his hand. She held it for a few minutes before informing him. "I'll see ya tomorrow. I hope you're havin' sweet dreams."

On her third day of caring for Thomas, Jinx bounced into the recovery area and plopped down beside him. "Howdy, Thomas. It's Jinx again. I brought another copy of the newspaper and I'm gonna read ya a good article today." She flipped through several pages before settling on an article. "I know I'm supposed to be studying my geography, so don't tell my mama. Okay?" She studied him carefully. His face was still pale, his body motionless. Then she leaned in closer. *I think his eyes are dartin' around under his eyelids. I better tell Nurse Ella.*

Jinx scanned the room but didn't see a nurse in sight, so she launched right into the newspaper article. "Jane Russell in *The Outlaw* is a big hit. Howard Hughes' acting discovery, Jane Russell, is the star of *The Outlaw*. The film concerns the exploits of Billy the Kid, but Miss Russell's cleavage somehow takes precedence over the plot." Jinx started giggling. "Her cleavage. Can ya believe they'd write 'bout cleavage in the newspaper?" Thomas didn't respond, and she continued. "The twenty-two-year-old actress hails from Minnesota." She smacked her leg elatedly. "Well, I'll be. I'm studying my geography after all. Right there," she pointed to the newspaper, "it says Minnesota." She glanced at her patient again and kept on reading. "There was a marked drop in commercial films this year. John Ford and Frank Capra are among several directors making public relations films for the Allied governments. John Huston's only work all year was the narration and direction of a picture called *Report from the A-leu-tians*. Jinx confessed. "I don't think I pronounced the last word correctly."

"You pronounced it just fine." She heard a soft voice.

Jinx's eyes popped. She stared at Thomas. "Did ya just say something?"

He nodded marginally.

"Hold on a minute." She told him. She rummaged around in her nurse's apron, pulled out her false teeth, and plunked them into her mouth. "Can ya open your eyes?"

Thomas' eyes slowly opened—just a tiny slit at first—then a little broader. She leaned in closer. "Welcome back!" She flashed him a wide smile.

He released a muted chuckle. "Thanks, kid."

"Wooo, Hooo!" She shouted as she began to twirl around in circles. "Thomas woke up! Thomas woke up!" Jinx chanted.

Applause and the echo of canes tapping on the floor erupted throughout the recovery room. "Way to go, Thomas!" She could hear someone call out. "Welcome back, buddy!" Another recuperating soldier chimed in.

"Let me go fetch Nurse Ella," she elatedly told her friend, "I'll be right back."

The next day, when she was making her rounds, she stopped in to visit Thomas. "How are ya doin'? I'm so glad ya woke up. I was prayin' for ya every night. Plus, today I brought ya some chocolate chip cookies straight from the oven, just like I promised."

"Thank you, Jinx." He motioned for her to come closer.

She leaned in and he whispered in her ear, "Are you going to tell me the story about Jack's mama at the waterin' hole?"

"You betcha." Her eyes sparkled mischievously.

Jam for the General

Jam for the General
January 1944

———— ❧ ————

"I'm here to deliver this tea and scones to the General," Jinx announced to the FBI agents who were stationed outside the door.

"I wasn't aware he ordered tea."

"Look, I gotta be honest with ya here. My mama told me to deliver this tray to the General and if I go back to the kitchen and still have this tray in my hands she's gonna beat me with a wooden spoon."

The sizeable man glared at her doubtfully.

"It's a big spoon, too," she added with a nod of her head.

"Two minutes." He jiggled the doorknob raucously before twisting it open and allowing her to enter.

She immediately slid her false teeth from her pocket and popped them into her mouth. "How ya doin', General?"

"I've been better," he answered, not bothering to open his eyes.

"Is there anything else I can fetch for ya? I've got some specialty tea my mama made and some scones. The tea has a touch of Saint John's Wort to soothe your worries and the strawberry jam is homemade. I helped Mama can it last week. It's the first time I ever made jam and I will admit it's pretty darn good."

He rolled over and stared at the young lady, startled when he noticed her mouthful of contorted teeth, and broke out in an appreciate laugh. "How old are you?"

"Fourteen."

His brow narrowed. "Really?"

"Alright. I'm thirteen and a half, but fourteen sounds so much more grown up. Don't ya think?"

"Do you work here?"

"No, but my mama does. However, I'm an Honorary Junior Nurse, so rest assured you're in good hands." She pointed to the very important Red Cross pin on her nurse's cap and nodded confidently. "Would ya like me to pour ya a cuppa tea and spread some jam on a scone for ya?"

"Did you say it was strawberry jam?"

"Yes, sir."

"That sounds very good. I can't recall the last time I had homemade strawberry jam."

Jinx carefully poured a cup of tea, smothered a scone with jam and placed it on the pivoting tray. She scooted it in close to him.

"What's your name?" the General asked.

"Jinx."

"You have a very unusual name." He took a nibble of the delicacy. "This is tasty."

"Can I ask ya something?"

He gestured for her to continue as he gobbled down the sweet treat.

"Is it ever gonna be peaceful and calm again? I have friends I met when the diplomats were staying here at the Greenbrier. Their names are Hinata and Aiko and they live in Japan. I don't know if you've been to Japan or happened to meet 'em, but I worry 'bout 'em and hope they're safe. Plus, I fret over my friend Sammy. He's in the Navy overseas somewhere." She woefully sighed.

"These are turbulent times."

"Ya know, when Hinata and Aiko were stayin' here, the government took all their money, which I didn't think was fair 'cause it wasn't like they started the war."

"Injustice is difficult to comprehend."

"Exactly," she refreshed his cup of tea, "the Germans were making fun of my friends in the dining room and I told them Germans exactly what

I thought—right to their face." Jinx recalled the day with perfect clarity. "Unfortunately, when my mama heard 'bout it she whacked me with a wooden spoon."

"Whacked you?"

"Yep. I was using barn language."

"Oh, I see."

"It really wasn't my fault, though. I might be a little pup, but I couldn't just stand around and do nothing when they were mocking my friends, right?"

"No," he agreed, "what counts is not necessarily the size of the dog in the fight—it's the size of the fight in the dog."

Jinx considered this for a moment. "That's a good sayin', General. I might borrow it sometime. Ya outta use it yourself in one of your speeches."

His forehead creased as he thought it all through. "I just might."

"Well, ya best polish off your tea. My mama will be lookin' for me and the FBI agents told me I only had two minutes to visit with ya." She earnestly informed him, "They don't have much of a sense of humor."

"I know." He gulped down the last bite of scone and washed it down with the hot tea.

"Alrighty then, I just snuck in here to see if ya knew when this mess would be sorted out. I figured if anybody had an answer, it'd be you."

"I am working diligently, I promise."

Jinx caught her lower lip between her lips as she got up the nerve to ask him. "Would ya care to autograph my book? Eleanor gave it to me on my sixth birthday and I've been collecting signatures ever since."

"Sure."

She handed him the very notable book.

He examined it carefully. Turning each page and reading the inscriptions one page at a time. When he reached the last message he let out a low whistle. "This is a very impressive collection of autographs you have here, Jinx."

"Well," she puffed up, "I do know some important folks."

"I would say so," he chuckled.

"Here, use this pen."

The General seemed to deliberate on what to write before he added his insightful words:

For Jinx,
Always remember…
Peace and justice are two sides of the same coin.
General Dwight D. Eisenhower
January '44.

"Thanks for the autograph, General. Keep workin' on our peace problem. Okay?"

"I will not stop until there is peace and justice in this world."

She tucked her book inside her apron and picked up the tray. "It was a pleasure meetin' ya, sir."

"You too, Jinx, and thanks for the jam."

"General?"

"Yes?"

Still not realizing how big the world really was, Jinx requested. "If you're over in Japan and run into Hinata and Aiko will ya tell 'em I said hello?"

"Absolutely," he promised.

"So, you were an Honorary Junior Nurse during the war," I recapped. "It must have been tough on you as a young teenager."

"You know, Dee, it was difficult times during the war but I enjoyed every moment."

"Tell me, Jinx, what did you like the most?"

"One of my favorite memories was when the soldier, Thomas, woke up. I was really concerned about him. He later told me he could hear me talking while he was sleeping and thought I could hear him talking back. He dreamed he had gone to heaven, until he opened his eyes and saw my crooked-toothed smile." She chuckled. "He even signed my book before he left the Greenbrier and advised me to always 'Take time to live in the present,' which now I realize was very wise advice."

"It is interesting that people can hear sounds and even voices when they are unconscious."

"I have found it is extremely important to talk to folks when they are in a state of unconsciousness. It doesn't matter if they can't respond. I know for a fact they can still hear the voices and noises going on around them." Jinx crossed her arms and propped her feet up on a short stool. "So, in addition to Thomas waking up, the day Sammy came home from the war was one of the best days of my life. He was honorably discharged from the Navy on September thirteenth in 1944, and ten days later he visited us at the Greenbrier. The ole rotten fellow didn't even laugh at my teeth. He just said he was glad Dr. Burl was able to improve my smile. I punched him hard on his arm." She laughed at her own memory and I joined in, truly appreciating her lighthearted sense of humor. "He later rejoined the staff and worked at the Greenbrier for years."

"Snead was one of the top players in the world for years, wasn't he?"

"He was an outstanding golf player for almost four decades."

"What happened to the Greenbrier after the war?"

"On the sixth day of August in 1945, an American B-29 bomber dropped the world's first deployed atomic bomb over the Japanese city of Hiroshima. The explosion killed more than ninety percent of the people instantly, and tens of thousands more would later die from radiation poisoning. I cried for days worrying about Hinata and Aiko." Her shoulders slumped. "I have no idea what became of them. Then, ten days later the war ended. There was a big celebration here at the Greenbrier. Thousands of people came to rejoice alongside the soldiers. That summer General Eisenhower was staying in the Top Notch cottage with his wife, and I happened to see him on the porch of the cottage. There was a famous sculptor creating a bronze casting of the General. The bronze bust is still on display over in the North Parlor. You should make sure you stop and see it." She added a carefree titter, "Sorry, I got sidetracked. Anyway, when I saw the General and his wife out on the porch

I hollered, 'Hey, General! How ya doin'?' He waved at me and shouted, 'Hi, Jinx. Come over here and meet my wife, Mamie.' I scampered over, so excited that he had remembered my name, and I had the opportunity to meet his lovely wife."

"He remembered your name? Astonishing."

"I've heard he had an excellent memory, and from my own experience would have to say it was true."

"He was an amazing man."

"I'm sure you are aware he later became the thirty-fourth President of the United States."

"It was a little before my time but I am aware of his distinguished accomplishments."

The elderly woman abruptly changed the conversation. "Ashford General Hospital was officially shut down in June of 1946. I had just turned sixteen and can recall the details as if they happened only yesterday. There was a touching flag-lowering ceremony on the day the hospital closed. I cried for days because I knew things would be changing again." She pointed at me to emphasize her point. "I was correct. In December, the government sold the hotel and grounds back to the Chesapeake and Ohio Railroad. Only a few weeks later, Mrs. Dorothy Draper arrived."

"Who is Dorothy Draper?"

Designing with Dorothy

Designing with Dorothy
December 1946

———— ❧ ————

A BRISK BREEZE whistled through the trees as it ushered in skies of blinding azure clarity. Mrs. Dorothy Draper had arrived earlier that morning and Sibert was already running his hand through his hair.

"What's wrong Sibert?" Jinx asked, as she bounced into the kitchen.

"Everything is wrong. We're working with a skeleton staff. I've been wheeling Mrs. Draper around in a wheelchair with her crutches balanced on her lap because she sprained her ankle, we have a leak in the gas line so we can't make tea or coffee, and she called our hotel, 'A Brobdingnagian monster of a bowling alley,'" he replied.

"Is Brobdingnagian a real word?"

"I have no idea."

"Who hired her to decorate our hotel anyway?"

"Robert R. Young, the Chairman of the Board of the C&O gave her carte blanche and now she wants everything to be 'Romance and Rhododendrons.'"

"Why rhododendrons?"

"I have no idea. She has asked me at least three times what our state flower is and I've replied the same way every single time. She always says the same thing, 'Rhododendron, a particular favorite of mine.' Jinx, she even suggested the murals in the Virginia Room be torn down and huge, wide, peppermint stripes be painted on the walls."

"Tear down the murals that were painted by William Grauer? Those murals took him over a year to paint!" Sixteen-year-old Jinx was an expert on the history of the Greenbrier and already decided she didn't much care for Mrs. Dorothy Draper's ideas. "I realize the diplomats would miss the dart board sometimes and there are a few holes in the murals but… "

"I know." Sibert shook his head remorsefully. "I'm going to sleep here tonight in case she needs anything."

"Mama and I can stay here tonight if ya want us to. Dr. Burl is at some sort of convention for dentists."

"You can ask her," he replied distractedly. "I need to make sure the gas line is fixed."

Later the same evening, Jinx and her mama were sitting in the kitchen drinking cold, day-old sweet tea when Sibert popped his head in the door. "The gas line is working again."

"Great. I'll brew us up some hot tea and bake some biscuits."

"Thank you." He replied wearily before disappearing again.

Jinx and her mama settled into a chilly room in the North Portico, right beside of Sibert's room. A few minutes after midnight they heard a knock on the door, followed by a low voice. "It's Sibert. Will you let me in?"

Jinx stumbled out of bed and ushered him in.

"You're not going to believe this one." He looked from one pair of sleepy eyes to the other. "Mrs. Draper just dialed the night desk and asked them to ring me. When I finally got dressed and knocked on her door she told me she thought someone had been in her room. Then she said it must have been a dream. Geez. She is going to drive me to drink." He bristled before running his hand through his hair. "Would you mind terribly to brew her up a pot of tea to help her sleep? Then maybe I can get some sleep."

"No problem," Jinx's mama answered as she tied the belt around her robe, "it will take me a few minutes."

Jinx followed her mama down the long corridor and into the kitchen where she commenced to infuse several ingredients together. "What kind of tea are ya makin', Mama?"

"Dream Tea," she replied.

"What's in it?"

"It is a blend of peppermint leaf, Chamomile flower, Gotu Kola, Mugwort, Rose petals, Sage and Rosemary. It should help Mrs. Draper sleep and it conjures up powerful and colorful dreams that are easily recalled."

"Would ya like me to take it to her?"

"Yes, thank you."

Jinx carried the tray to Mrs. Draper's room and knocked twice on the door.

"Some settling tea for ya, ma'am," Jinx announced as she entered the room.

"Thank you. Please set it on the table."

She placed the tray on the table in the corner of the room. "Is there anything else ya need?"

"No," the woman replied, "but let me ask you a question. Have you ever seen a ghost here at the Greenbrier?"

"A ghost?" Jinx thought this through. "Nope. Not here at the Greenbrier. However, there is the tale of Zona Heaster Shue who was murdered by her husband. They lived around here somewhere. The legend says an errand boy found Zona's body and by the time the coroner arrived, which was around an hour later, her husband had laid her out on the bed and was dressing the corpse himself in a high-necked dress with a stiff collar and had placed a veil over her face. When the coroner noticed bruising on her neck and tried to look closer, her husband started screaming and shouting at the coroner and told him to get out of their house." Jinx leaned in closer. "Do ya wanna hear the rest of the story?"

"I'm not sure this is going to help me sleep any better," Mrs. Draper replied.

"Well," Jinx continued, "Zona appeared to her mama in a dream a few weeks after the funeral, and told her that her husband had killed her in a fit of rage 'cause she hadn't cooked him meat for dinner. He broke her neck. Zona's head turned around backwards so her mama would believe her story." Jinx slowly rotated her head as far as possible before abruptly and dramatically snapping it back. Her voice lowered to a whisper. "She kept visiting her mama night after night until her mama finally believed her."

Mrs. Draper's wide eyes were staring entrancedly at the young girl.

"Zona's mama started tellin' folks what happened so they dug up her body to examine it."

"They *exhumed* her body." Mrs. Draper corrected.

"That's not the way I heard it." Jinx rolled her eyes. "But anyway, her mama testified in court and the murderer was found guilty and sentenced to life in prison."

"He was found guilty based on her mother's testimony?"

"Yep. Since Zona's ghost appeared to her mama her husband was found guilty." She leaned in close to Mrs. Draper. "Folks say if ya talk 'bout Zona's death at nighttime she'll come and visit ya."

Mrs. Draper leaned back and pressed her hand on her forehead. "That is a very strange story."

"Yep, it is. Can ya believe all that happened just 'cause she didn't fry up some chicken for dinner?" Jinx looked over her shoulder as though she were examining the room for signs of Zona materializing. She gawked at the area beneath the bed before whispering, "Ya haven't seen a ghost have ya, Mrs. Draper?"

"I don't think so," she sighed. "I thought I did, though. I must have been dreaming, because I could have sworn Robert E. Lee was mounted on his horse at the foot of my bed."

The sixteen-year-old stifled a giggled. *Robert E. Lee? On a horse? In the Greenbrier?* "You're probably just stressed from your travels. Let me pour ya a cuppa tea. My mama made it. She's the Tea Master here and this is one of her specialty blends. It's called Dream Tea and it will help ya sleep and have beautiful dreams."

Mrs. Draper accepted the cup and sipped it daintily. "Would you mind staying for a few minutes and talking with me?"

"Sure." Jinx plopped down on an overstuffed chair facing the woman. "Do ya have any experience decorating large hotels?" she asked, as if she were interviewing Mrs. Draper for the job.

"Oh yes, I have a great deal of experience. I am a well-known interior decorator. I have decorated the Carlyle Hotel on Madison Avenue, New York's Sutton Place, the Fairmont and Mark Hopkins Hotel... " she flipped her hand nonchalantly, "I have transformed many less than desirable buildings into fabulous works of art." She poured herself another cup of Dream Tea. "Do you know what the state flower is?"

Now, Jinx already knew Sibert had conveyed this information to her multiple times and briefly wondered if the woman had a memory problem. So she intentionally decided to pull her leg. "The official state flower or the unofficial state flower?"

"There is an unofficial state flower? I had no idea. What is it?"

"Forget-me-nots." It was the first thing that popped into her head.

Dorothy Draper considered this judiciously. "Are forget-me-nots blue or purple?" She seemed to search her memory. "Are they the shade of cobalt?"

I don't have a clue. Jinx silently reflected before offering up, "They come in different shades—blue, turquoise, purple and perhaps cobalt," she replied straight-faced. "I think."

"Splendid." Mrs. Draper yawned. "What is your name?"

"My name is Jinx."

"Would you mind bringing me another pot of this delicious tea again tomorrow night?"

"If it's before midnight."

Mrs. Draper glanced at the clock. "Of course, my apologies. Would eight o'clock be acceptable?"

"Yes, ma'am."

"Thank you, young lady."

"So," Sibert announced to Jinx and her mama, as he shuffled into the kitchen on the following morning, "Mrs. Draper wants to decorate the entire hotel in hunting pink and fuchsia, lime and hunter green, cobalt blue and turquoise. She said the idea of cobalt blue and turquoise came to her because forget-me-nots were the *unofficial* state flower. Have you ever heard of such a ridiculous notion? An unofficial state flower."

"That's a hoot," Jinx smacked her leg elatedly, "the unofficial state flower."

Sibert and her mama looked at her questioningly as a cup of hot Chamomile tea was slid across the table. "Would you like a shot of brandy, Sibert?"

"I'd like one but I'm working," he muttered before taking a sip of the steaming tea. "She also wants to strip the antiques and paint them black." He winced at the very thought. "Only a Yankee would paint antique mahogany furniture black."

"Sibert," her mama advised, "you just need to stop worrying over this."

"She wants to remove the historic chaperones' balcony from the ballroom. She said it was an anachronism."

"Is anachronism a real word?" Jinx asked.

"Yes, it means a relic or a remnant from the past." He gloomily reported, "Plus, she wants us to add low-calorie choices to our menu."

Everyone groaned in unison.

Jinx carried her autograph book and tray full of tea and cookies into Mrs. Draper's room. "I was hoping you'd be able to autograph the book Eleanor Roosevelt gave me on my sixth birthday."

"Eleanor Roosevelt?"

"Yep. She's my friend."

"Really?" Dorothy poured a cup of tea. "She is my friend, too."

"Well, I'll be. Did she ever tell ya 'bout her mother-in-law? One time her mother-in-law told her she'd look so much nicer if she'd run a comb through her hair." Jinx pursed her lips. "I didn't think it was a very kind thing to say."

Dorothy knowingly nodded. "I can believe it. I knew Eleanor's mother-in-law and I admit I am very grateful I wasn't related to her." She paused to take a drink of tea. "I also had a similar incident one time. Years ago, my aunt had seen me without my makeup and lipstick on at the Palm Court in New York City. She promptly wrote me a letter to inform me that I should never go out in public without my face made-up."

"Really?" Jinx shook her head. "Sometimes people tell folks things that are really none of their business."

"For sure."

"So," Jinx asked, "how do ya know Eleanor?"

"We were neighbors when we lived in Tuxedo Park. I recall Eleanor telling me an access door had been installed between their brownstone and her mother-in-law's. The woman would often burst through the double doors of the dining room unexpectedly and scrutinize how Eleanor was dressed or how she was raising her children, and since her husband was working all the time, she was often alone with her mother-in-law and children for weeks on end." Her finger rose into the air as if she suddenly recalled an important point. "Nonetheless, Eleanor promptly realized she should become involved with charity and women's issues and put her energy into making the world a better place. Eleanor is a very intelligent woman."

"Yep." Jinx nodded.

"Coincidentally, Eleanor and I both ended up moving to Washington, D.C. and still often speak on the telephone or meet for lunch when time allows."

Jinx shifted in her seat uncomfortably before asking Dorothy. "Do ya really think it is a good idea to remove historic chaperones' balcony from the ballroom?"

"They are old fashioned and I am revamping."

"Do ya think puttin' in wide stripes of paint over the murals is a smart idea?"

"I always put in one controversial item. It makes people talk."

"Controversial? Do ya mean like the Duchess of Windsor?"

"Do you know the duchess?" Dorothy's interest piqued.

"Yep. Wallis is my friend."

"Wallis?"

"Yep. That's what she told me to call her. Anyway, folks were talkin' 'bout her when she was involved in the scandal."

"The duchess was involved in a scandal?" She leaned in closer. "Do tell."

Jinx offered up her version of the story. "Oh, Wallis fell in love with King Edward the Eighth, and he fell in love with her. Regrettably, she was married to someone else, then she filed for a divorce so she could marry King Edward and the church didn't like it."

"Oh," Dorothy leaned back in her chair, "I am aware of this particular scandal."

Jinx flipped through the pages of her prized journal. "Wallis signed my book."

"Let me see." She practically snatched the book out of her hands. When Dorothy read the inscription aloud, "A woman can't be too rich or too thin. But just in case ~ always wear your under panties," she let out an appreciative laugh. She skimmed through a few more pages. "Oh, you are friends with Clare Boothe Luce, too?"

"Yep."

"Quite impressive. She is also a friend of mine." She picked up the Golden Herringbone fountain pen, which Eleanor had bestowed to Jinx and jiggled it in her hand for a moment before writing her important message in the embossed leather journal.

For Jinx,
Controversy makes people talk ~ which is not always a bad thing.
Dorothy Draper
January '47

Day after day the controversy continued. One fall morning in 1947, Sibert stormed into the kitchen. "You're not going to believe this one," he announced as he dropped down into the chair.

"What?" Jinx and her mama asked in unison.

"Mrs. Draper ordered the grounds crew to cut down the oak tree out front." He cringed.

"She wants to cut down the tree?" Jinx gasped.

"Yes, she said it obstructed the view of the hotel and called it offending."

"Offending? It's a four-hundred-year-old tree!"

"I know." He ran his fingers through his hair. "I don't know if I'm going to survive this."

Jinx's mama comforted him. "You'll survive, Sibert. Let's face it. We made it through the visiting diplomats, the hospital, and the prisoners of war staying here at the Old White. This too shall pass."

Jinx joined in. "She did renege on covering up the murals in the Virginia Room."

"True. But listen to this one. She wants to *redress* the staff. She wants them to wear costumes."

"Costumes?"

"Yes, she has designed red shirts and green caps for the caddies, added ornate round buttons to the doormen's and porter's new red and green uniforms and wants Big Florence to were a *mammy* costume with hoops, and lace petticoats. The parlor maids now have a short-skirted version of Big Florence's costume and they can't even bend over to clean up the rooms. It is one hot mess. The problems are mounting and the original date of the reopening has been postponed until each detail is ironed out."

"Postponed? Until when?"

"Next spring." Sibert sadly reported. "It may be six more months."

"So, Dee," Jinx nudged me, "after spending over a year occasionally having tea with Dorothy Draper, I learned so much about designing interiors. She paid great attention to details—down to the color of the washcloths and scent of the soap in each of the bathrooms." She confided, "Though she nearly drove Sibert insane."

I could easily comprehend how much Mrs. Dorothy Draper had impressed Jinx during their time together—all those years ago.

"If you have the chance, make sure you visit the Victorian Writing Room. It is lovely, with its green walls, fuchsia carpet, and gold chandelier. It has remained unchanged after all these years, and the forget-me-not colors in the main lobby always make me smile."

"The Greenbrier Hotel is an amazing place," I admitted.

"The entire hotel was *Draperized* with a total of thirty miles of carpeting, forty-five-thousand yards of fabric, and fifteen-thousand rolls of wallpaper."

"Did they cut down the oak tree?"

"They finally talked Dorothy out of chopping down the tree after disagreeing on the topic for months. Just as the men were turning on the power saw a compromise was made. Several smaller trees were transplanted but the giant oak remained." She thoughtfully added, "However, Dorothy finally won the battle of the offending oak tree when the hotel removed it in 1987."

"Whether she was cantankerous or not, she was clearly a gifted designer."

"She really was an amazing woman. She led a high life with high style and demanded perfection."

Two weeks before the Grand Reopening up the Greenbrier, Dr. Burl insisted they drive to Charleston to buy Jinx a gown for the Diamond Ball. "Jinx will attend the ball and she will look as elegant and fashionable as the Duchess of Windsor, Mrs. Draper, or the Kennedy sisters."

So, on Saturday morning Dr. Burl, Jinx, and her mama piled into the royal blue Dodge Sedan and made the three-hour drive to the Diamond Department Store. Dr. Burl easily found a parking place directly in front of the tall building on Capitol Street. "It looks as if they have added a few floors to this building since I was here last winter," he told them as they were walking into the store. "I think I'll go to the snack bar and order a soda while you ladies shop. Remember, you can get any dress you find. It doesn't matter how much it costs." He leaned in close to his wife. "I want you to find something, too."

Jinx and her mama scanned the young miss department and didn't find anything they felt would be a suitable fit for the Diamond Ball, so they took the elevator to the fifth floor and perused the ladies fine apparel department. Jinx noticed her mama pause to examine a mustard-yellow two piece set. A matching blouse with a long tie hanging from the neckline complemented the waspy-waist full-skirt. Her eyes skimmed the price tag. "Twelve dollars for each piece?" Her hand immediately dropped to her side. "Pricey." She quickly spotted the evening wear and realized that, due to Jinx's petite structure, they would have to choose from ten possible gowns. "We may as well take them all in the dressing room and try every one of them on."

"I need one with a pocket in it," Jinx informed her.

"You're not taking those ridiculous teeth to the ball. I wish Dr. Burl would quit making them for you."

"Of course I'm not wearing my false teeth to the ball, Mama." Jinx rolled her eyes. "I just need a pocket."

"Try this one on." She handed her an emerald green slipper satin gown. Jinx slid it on and when she stepped out of the dressing area her mama gasped. She ushered back into the changing area. "Oh, dear. Your cleavage is bursting out over the top."

Jinx's face contorted. "Cleavage? I ain't got no cleavage, Mama. What are ya talkin' 'bout?"

"You don't have any cleavage."

"That's what I said."

"No, you said you ain't got no cleavage and I thought you were trying to erase the word ain't from your vocabulary."

"Let's face it, Mama, no matter how I say it the truth remains the same. The training bra experiment was a total flop."

She offered a half smile before holding her hand up. "You are not wearing this dress out in public." She tossed her another gown. "Try this one."

The wine-colored soft crepe gown hung on her like an extra-large bath towel on a three-day-old bar of soap. "No, you'd need to put on fifty pounds for this one to look nice on you. " Her mama shook her head as she handed her the next one.

Seven dresses and fifty-five minutes later, Jinx found the one. It was a pink ball gown with little faux diamonds situated around the neckline, and the exaggerated full skirt, which was made out of taffeta, was the perfect length. A matching stole could be draped over her shoulders and, much to Jinx's disbelief; it even had a tiny pocket on the right side of the waistline. When she stepped from the dressing area, her mama and Dr. Burl were standing there.

"I thought you ladies had left me," Dr. Burl glimpsed at his watch, "I've been waiting for almost two hours and if I drink one more soda pop I'm going to bust."

Jinx laughed and twirled around for him. "What do ya think? Is the dress classy, Dr. Burl?"

"Jinx, you look truly lovely."

"You look beautiful." Her mama whispered. "You remind me of your papa with your blonde hair, green eyes, and thin physique. You're the spitting image of him."

"Thank ya, Mama."

"How long do you think it will take you to find some shoes?" Dr. Burl timidly inquired.

Her mama placed her hand on his arm. "We'll be quick." She pecked him on the cheek. "Thanks, sweetie."

He gave her a wink.

"Why don't ya try on the yellow outfit, Mama? It would look mighty attractive on ya."

"Absolutely not," she shook her head. "It is too expensive. Plus, we are shopping for you."

"Which yellow dress?" Dr. Burl asked, as he scanned the hundreds of dresses displayed around the room.

Jinx walked over to the mustard-yellow outfit and handed it to her. "Go try it on."

"It's very expensive, Jinx."

"Well, I'd rather ya buy a new dress that ya'd wear all the time, instead of gettin' one for me. Really Mama, I'm only gonna wear this dress once, maybe twice."

"Ladies," Dr. Burl insisted, "we can afford them both." His attention turned toward his wife. "Please try it on."

Jinx noticed her mama's eyes were brimming with tears. "Well, if you're sure."

"I am insisting."

By the time they checked out of the Diamond Department Store, Jinx had her first evening gown, complete with a matching stole, ruffle-cuffed gloves, and shell ankle-strap shoes, and her mama now owned a classy mustard-yellow two piece suit… most likely the finest outfit she had ever possessed.

When Dr. Burl opened the passenger side door for her mama to slide into the front seat Jinx whispered in his ear. "Don't tell Mama this, but my gown has a secret pocket so I can smuggle my false teeth into the ball."

He bit his lip. "Your mama's going to kill me, Jinx."

Dr. Burl was as proud as a peacock, Jinx could tell by the lopsided grin on his face. All the way home she kept thinking about how lucky they were to have Dr. Burl in their lives. She recalled learning in church that it was better to give than to receive and she figured this was why Dr. Burl felt so proud. As they zoomed along in the royal blue Dodge Sedan, she gazed out the window watching the dogwoods and sugar maples reawakening in the spring sunshine. Her thoughts drifted to her papa and she wondered if her mama still missed him as much as she did.

When Dr. Burl broke out singing "Golden Earrings" by Peggy Lee, her mama started singing along—completely off-key.

It was the sweetest song Jinx had ever heard.

The Grand Reopening

The Grand Reopening
April 1948

———❧———

ONE YEAR AND four months after Dorothy Draper arrived, the Greenbrier Hotel was complete. A grand reopening was scheduled. It would take place from April fifteenth through the eighteenth and simply *everyone* was invited. There was a new excitement in the air. Mr. and Mrs. Robert E. Young, the Duke and Duchess of Windsor, William Morrow, Bing Crosby, Rose and Joseph, Jack and Eunice, Patricia, and Kathleen Kennedy, the Aldriches, the Astors, the Binghams, and the Vanderbilts were in attendance. The Duponts, the Floyds, the Van Burens, and the Van Pelts made an appearance—just to name a few. It was truly the gathering of the elite, powerful, rich and famous.

Camera and editorial crews from *Life, Time, Harper's Bazaar, Vogue* and *Esquire* were ready to report the festivities of the weekend, and more specifically, to present to the world the *newly redecorated* Greenbrier Hotel.

On the day before the hotel was to open, Dorothy was making her final inspections. When she sniffed the soap in the duchess' bathroom, she barked, "This is not what I ordered. The scent is wrong!" She huffed and puffed.

When she saw Jinx and her mama standing outside of the Cameo Ballroom, admiring the new chandelier that was just unveiled, she pointedly addressed the other woman. "The scent of the soap in the duchess' bathroom is not what I ordered."

"I'll see if I can find someone to replace it." Jinx's mama replied calmly.

"You will see *if* you can find someone to replace it?" Her eyes narrowed and her voice rose in volume. "We will not open until this scent fiasco is corrected."

Jinx stepped forward and intentionally positioned herself between Mrs. Draper and her mama and crossed her arms in front of her chest. "My mama is the Tea Master here at the hotel. Her job doesn't entail ordering soap." She tilted her head defiantly.

"So," Dorothy cleared her throat, "dare tell, who is the Soap Master here?" The sarcasm dripped from her tongue.

Jinx could feel her face heating up. She knew she needed to calm herself down. She took in a deep breath. "I wouldn't pee… pee… presume to know who is in charge of ordering soap." She was, of course, fibbing.

"Jinx, I realize you know everything that is going on around here and I believe you can help me," Dorothy said mildly.

"Sorry," Jinx shrugged her shoulders, "I have no idea."

Sibert turned the corner just in time to see Mrs. Draper, with her hands propped on her hips, and Jinx, with her arms folded in front of her chest. Behind Jinx, Sibert could see, was her mama. Sibert could tell, by the staunch position Jinx had assumed, that prompt intervention was needed. "Is there a problem, ladies?"

Dorothy Draper swiftly turned to face him. "This hotel will not open until the soap in the duchess' bathroom is replaced. The scent is despicable."

"Please," he started guiding her away, "show me what the problem is."

When they had turned the corner, Jinx's mama whispered, "Thanks for not telling her you wouldn't pee on her if she was on fire."

"And take the risk of getting beat with a wooden spoon again? I don't think so."

"Beat?" Her mama rolled her eyes dismissively. "I barely grazed you."

"That's not how I remember it."

"Well, Jinx, you do have quite an imagination." She grabbed her hand. "Let me brew you a cup of tea."

Jinx stayed at the hotel late that night working at the check-in desk. Freddie, the desk cashier during the day, had methodically arranged the reservations and they were in impeccable order. Jinx regretted having to create chaos and mayhem, especially since Freddie was so remarkably efficient. *But, a girl has to do what a girl has to do.*

Jinx was trying to recall every malicious article she had recently read in the tabloid magazines while searching through the list of guests who were scheduled to arrive the following morning. She checked and double-checked room assignments. At two o'clock in the morning she figured she had made appropriate arrangements. She was going to get revenge on Mrs. Dorothy Draper, because no one was going to speak to her mama the way Dorothy attempted to earlier in the day. *Dorothy Draper acting all hoity-toity.* The tone of voice she used when addressing her mama kept rolling through Jinx's mind. *Dare tell, who is the Soap Master here.* "Humph!"

The following morning, Rolls-Royces, special trains and planes arrived at the gates of the Greenbrier delivering the famous guests. At the front desk there were lines of celebrities, news reporters, and government officials waiting to be escorted to their rooms.

The first hint of confusion came when publishing czar Mr. William Randolph Hearst, and his new bride, arrived in their quarters only to find the previous Mrs. Hearst had already settled in. The couple had divorced recently, Jinx knew, so she figured having a husband with his ex-wife and new bride assigned to the same room would trigger Dorothy Draper to gasp in sheer horror.

It did.

The next mix-up came with society reporters. Mr. Igor Cassini walked into his room with his new wife only to find that his former wife, Bootsie, occupied it. Again, another screech of distress escaped from the lips of Mrs. Draper. The madness continued as ex-husbands, ex-wives, and ex-wives of ex-husbands found themselves assigned to the same rooms.

"Jinx!" Sibert called out.

She took off running toward the golf course, hoping to give Sibert some time to calm down, and spied Sammy talking to Bing Crosby and a reporter from *Life* magazine.

"Hey there, Sammy." Jinx approached him from behind and wiggled through the crowd in an attempt to shield herself from Sibert's view.

"Come here, Jinx." Sammy motioned for her to join them. "I want you to meet somebody. This is Mr. Bing Crosby."

"It's a pleasure to meet ya, sir."

"Likewise, Jinx."

Sammy explained, "Jinx and I have been friends since she was six years old. She practically lives here at Greenbrier since her mama is employed as the Tea Master."

Bing's eyes widened. "You are one lucky gal—living at the Greenbrier is a dream come true. You should count your blessings, babe. This is one high-class place. I had to wash and iron my shirt before sending it to the laundry."

Jinx giggled. "I count my blessings every day."

"Are you a movie star?" Bing asked.

"Not yet."

"Are you eighteen?"

"No, she is not." Sammy answered for her.

"I bet the young men around these parts are buzzing around you like bees on honey. Is your dance card full for the Diamond Ball yet? If not, please save me a dance."

"I'll try to fit ya in," Jinx told him.

He gave her a quick wink.

"Do ya have time to sign my autograph book? Eleanor Roosevelt gave it to me on my sixth birthday."

"Absolutely. Let me try to think of something insightful to convey."

So while the men were standing around, waiting to tee off, Bing Crosby wrote:

To Jinx,

When I'm worried and I can't sleep,

I count my blessings instead of sheep.

And I fall asleep…

Counting my blessings.

Bing Crosby

April '48

The next day, the royal couple of America arrived. Jinx knew Dorothy Draper would be perched at the window directly above the porte-cochere, where she could watch the front door. She had decorated the suite for the Duke and Duchess of Windsor expressly for the duchess' tastes, with sprigs of violets and soft purples and would be anxious to discover if the duchess approved. The couple made Dorothy nervous and Jinx knew this, so she called out, "Hey, duchess!"

The duchess turned and waved back. "Hello, Jinx."

This was all Jinx wanted Mrs. Dorothy Draper to see. *Yep, Wallis was her friend.*

The press counted the forty-two pieces of luggage they had brought with them as they made their way to the Presidential Suite, and even though the reporters were asking never-ending questions as they made the short jaunt to their quarters, Jinx was the only one who received a response.

The days went by quickly and throughout the entire time Jinx held tight to her beloved journal. She managed to get autographs from Judy Garland, Meyer Davis, Rose Kennedy, William Morrow, and Grace Kelly's parents—just to name a few.

The climax of the merry weekend was the Diamond Ball, which was held on the third and final night of the party. It would, of course, be held in the Cameo Ballroom.

Early in the afternoon, Susan, who used to work at the Greenbrier before it was transformed into a hospital, came by the farmhouse and styled Jinx's hair. She shaped an elegant upswept coiffure with wispy sprays dangling just below Jinx's rosy cheeks. Dr. Burl and her mama hauled to the hotel her extravagantly full-skirted pink ball gown with little faux diamonds situated around the neckline. Jinx changed out of her homemade trousers and cotton blouse in the bathroom located beside of the employee's kitchen. She pulled on her ruffle-cuffed gloves, clasped on her ankle-strapped shell shoes, and tucked her false teeth into the hidden pocket.

Her mama brewed a cup of White tea with Royal jelly to enhance her self-confidence. "I doubt you really need a confidence booster, but take a few drinks of this tea, Jinx." She shoved a steaming cup across the table. "Always remember that you are as good as anyone. There will be movie stars, royalty, and wealthy folks at the ball tonight and you are as beautiful and as important as they are. So don't be afraid."

"I know," Jinx casually replied.

Jinx's mama shook her head. "I would be as nervous as a long-tailed cat in a room full of rocking chairs and you're as cool as a cucumber, so let me say right here and now, I have no idea how I raised such a wonderfully, self-assured young lady."

She kissed her mama on the cheek, squared her shoulders and strolled like the Queen of Sheba toward the Cameo Ballroom. Two months before her eighteenth birthday, she entered the room with more poise than most adults. She easily found her table where Sammy and his wife were seated and snuggled in between them. Audrey leaned over and whispered, "I'm sure glad you didn't look like you do now when I was trying to lasso Sammy. The competition would have been stiff."

Jinx smiled shyly and patted Audrey on her hand. "Thank ya, but I realize now Sammy is much too old for me."

Audrey burst out laughing. "You have always been such a stinker."

The guests dined on Turtle Soup, caviar, English Pheasant with wild rice, Virginia ham smothered in mushrooms, accompanied by bubbling cava. After dinner there was a raffle to benefit the Salvation Army, then the Meyer Davis Orchestra started playing. Judy Garland was one of the first celebrities to perform and Bing Crosby, who had an ironclad rule against entertaining at parties, even crooned, "The Whiffenpoof Song" and "Now is the Time." The Duke of Windsor joined in and played the drums alongside bandleader, Meyer Davis.

Bing was correct when he had predicted the young men would be buzzing around Jinx like bees on honey. She had numerous requests to dance from every single man under the age of forty, and would occasionally accept their invitation—under Sammy's watchful eye, of course. When the band started playing the "Too Fat Polka" Sammy asked her to join him. Jinx suddenly recalled the advice that Ms. Alice, the maid who had taught her to dance, had bestowed upon her many years earlier. "You're going to need to know how to twirl gracefully when you start dancing with the boys." She was thankful she had listened.

Jinx strutted around like the queen of the ball. She complimented Wallis, the Duchess of Windsor, on her oyster white satin gown embroidered with crystals.

The duchess leaned in close and whispered. "You look lavish as well, Jinx."

"Thank ya, Wallis. You're just as thin as the last time I saw ya."

The duchess smiled before confiding. "Rest assured, I am wearing my under panties."

"Me too."

They shared a secret laugh and Jinx noticed Mrs. Dorothy Draper watching them with great interest.

Jinx overheard someone comment on the chandelier, insisting it had been there since the days of General Lee. She knew better than to correct them and went about being a social butterfly. She casually strolled over to the reporter from *Life* magazine and inquired as to whether he was planning to feature the Duke and Duchess of Windsor on the cover of the magazine.

"I was planning to use Mrs. Draper's photograph."

"Are ya kiddin' me?" She shook her head. "Everyone's gonna wanna to see the Duke and Duchess." Jinx knew Dorothy had created the magical evening and transformation of the hotel, and that she also desperately desired to be featured on the cover of *Life*. She was still trying to get Dorothy's goat for the way she had addressed her mama. *Dorothy Draper will be fit to be tied,* she thought as she scanned the room.

The party was great fun and the hours passed hurriedly. Then when the bandleader, Meyer Davis, announced that the last song of the evening was coming up, everyone stood to find a place on the parquet floor suspended on chains. Bing Crosby made his way over to Sammy Snead's table and addressed Jinx. "Did you save the last dance for me?"

"Yes, sir." She took his hand. As they were walking to the dance floor, she tugged her false teeth from the secret compartment of her skirt and popped them into her mouth.

"Sweet Sixteen," a song made popular by Perry Como, started resonating across the room. Jinx turned to face Bing and when she smiled at him, with her mouth chocked-full of crooked and blacked-out teeth, he startled, before bursting out in laughter. He couldn't stop himself. He doubled over and smacked his knee several times. Bing gasped—trying desperately to catch his breath. He started coughing and laughing at the same time. He was chuckling so hard that Jinx had to bang him hard on the back a few times to help him recover. He was still wiping away the tears from his eyes when he, once again, presented his hand to her. "May I dance with you, lovely lady?"

Meyer Davis and his orchestra were mesmerizing the crowd, as they tripped the light fantastic and sashayed across the floor.

She noticed Sibert, Freddie, and Ms. Alice watching from the doorway. Her mama and Dr. Burl had slipped into the ballroom and were proudly regarding the young woman dancing with the movie star. The doorman, Martin, tipped his hat at her from a corner of the room. Like a beauty queen in a sparkling dress, she offered a diminutive wave in return.

The Duchess of Windsor even imparted a quick wink as Bing twirled her through the crowd of the majestic Cameo Ballroom.

The crystal lights speckled and sent prisms of rainbows in every direction. The diamond-shaped sparkles pranced along Dorothy Draper's rhododendron-covered walls. An open promenade followed by a reverse pivot sent Jinx spinning away from her dance partner before he pulled her back and dipped her low.

"Jinx, I don't know if I have ever met such a delightful young lady," he said as he spun her under his arm—demonstrating ballroom fashion extraordinaire.

"Thank ya, sir."

"I sure wish you were eighteen years old," Bing teased.

"She's not!" Jinx heard Sammy bark.

After all the fanfare had died down, Jinx, Sibert, her mama, Dr. Burl, Ms. Alice, Freddie, Martin and Sammy where sitting around the table sipping tea. Jinx was scanning through a copy of *The Last Resorts.* "Look here, Sibert." She pointed to the picture of the Greenbrier Hotel before reciting the article aloud. "Cleveland Armory, one of America's most popular reporters of high society history eloquently reports, 'The affair at the Greenbrier Hotel was *the* outstanding resort Society function in modern history.'"

"Geez." Sibert ran his hand through his hair. "I wonder what's coming next."

"Little did Sibert know that ten years later the government would, once again, call upon the Greenbrier Hotel. In 1958 the plans to construct the secret underground bunker would begin."

"Were you here when the underground bunker was constructed?" I inquired.

"I was not here to witness the transformation of the Greenbrier into Project Casper, or what they later changed to Project Green Island, in its entirety. However, if you have time you may consider touring the facility."

"Maybe…" I considered the list of historically significant memorabilia I still wanted to see in the fabulous Greenbrier Hotel.

"The top-secret bunker is a story for another day." Jinx patted my arm before hurriedly changing the topic. "So Dee, those are the tales I wanted you to hear. These are stories of my childhood. The days I spent growing up at the Greenbrier." She continued, "College started another chapter in my life and I left the Greenbrier the following fall. Even though I attended college, and eventually married, I return every summer and this place still feels like home to me. When I visited during the summer months, I had the opportunity to meet presidents and celebrities like Bob Hope, John F. Kennedy, Richard

Nixon, Lyndon Johnson, Paul Harvey, Billy Graham, Debbie Reynolds, Eddie Fisher, Prince Rainier and Princess Grace."

"Wow."

"Dee, I'm just sharing some of the most memorable events of my early days. A decade packed full of unforgettable experiences and countless opportunities to chat with people whom most people would never have the opportunity to meet. You can use what you want and don't feel obligated to write any of my tales at all." Jinx explained. "I do hope you can remember everything I've told you."

I smiled politely.

"To good friends and good tales."

The distinct taste of Sulphur water and tea infused with Holy Basil lingered on my tongue.

"Bottoms up."

At the Greenbrier

At the Greenbrier
June 2016

———— ❧ ————

I woke up with a splitting headache, nuzzled snuggly under a warm blanket, lying in a fluffy bed with six pillows tucked around my head. The bright light shining through the window glowed on the pink and white striped wallpaper. I glanced around the room, taking in the floral upholstery covering the overstuffed chairs, exquisite French antiques, and soft Oriental rugs. I momentarily thought I had died and gone to heaven until I saw an exhausted looking woman in her early thirties, snoring in a chair beside my bed. The tag pinned on her scrubs indicated her name was Sally.

"Sally?" I whispered.

She didn't stir.

"Sally?" My voice rose marginally.

Still there was no response.

I slung a pillow at her causing her to abruptly startle from her wheezing state of slumber. "Well," she picked up a wad of gum that had fallen from her mouth and landed on her lap. She jammed it back into her mouth and commenced to vigorously chew, "welcome back, sweetie."

"Welcome back?" I repeated, noticeably in a foggy state of confusion.

"Yes, welcome back." She straightened, plucked a clipboard up from underneath her chair, and stared at me intensely. "Let me ask ya a couple questions."

"Okay."

"Do ya know the date?"

I have to be perfectly honest here. Although my undergraduate degree is in English, my graduate degrees are in psychology. I have spent many days in the psychiatric ward—as a therapist, not a patient. I am more than familiar with the queries used to determine whether or not someone should be admitted, and I sure didn't care for how this scene was progressing. I knew if Sally was following the correct protocol, she should be inquiring about such things as if I knew my name, where I was, the date, and who the current president of the United States was. Not necessarily in this order, mind you, but these questions should eventually be asked in the course of our conversation. I desperately tried to pull back the date. Finally, I confessed. "No, I do not know the exact date."

Sally discarded her mouth full of gum, snatched a foil-lined packet from her pocket, dispensed three pieces of Nicorette gum, and tossed them into her mouth. "I'm trying to quit smoking."

"Good for you."

"Okay, sweetie. Do ya know who the president of the United States is?" She clicked her ballpoint pen.

"Eleanor Roosevelt?" I knew it sounded more like a question than a definitive answer.

"In our dreams." Sally murmured as she located a remote and tapped the green button. CNN started blaring from a television that was resolutely positioned on a fashionable cabinet located in the far corner.

Visions of President Obama, Hillary Clinton, and Donald Trump flashed across the screen.

The Supreme Court announced on Thursday that it had deadlocked in a cast challenging President Obama's immigration plan, effectively ending what Mr. Obama had hope would become one of his central legacies. The program would have shielded as many as five million undocumented immigrants from deportation and allowed them to legally work in the United States.

Today's deadlocked decision from the Supreme Court is unacceptable, says Mrs. Clinton, and shows us all just how high the stakes are in this election. This decision is also a stark reminder of the harm Donald Trump would do to our families, our communities, and our country.

Donald Trump delivered a blistering attack this week against Hillary Clinton, calling her unreliable and more concerned with herself than with the American people as he sought to regain his footing after a tumultuous month that imperiled his candidacy.

"Oh, no!" I gasped. My hand rose to cover my mouth.

"Sorry, sweetie. I know it's scary. Ya most likely wish ya hadn't woke up now." Sally clicked the button to turn the television off.

"How did I get here?"

"Earl and Margie Stutler were sprucing up the community room when they heard your car wash up on the hillside right in front of the Free Will Baptist Church. They said it had been forced up by the floodwaters and ya ended up right smack-dab underneath the 'Jesus Saves' sign."

"I guess I was pretty lucky, eh?"

"Ya think? Somebody was definitely watching over ya. Apparently ya bumped your head. All the roads were flooded and they couldn't drive ya to the hospital, so they brought ya up here."

"Wow!" I meditated on this information momentarily. "Where's here?"

"You're at the Old White, or the Greenbrier Resort, as most of the world refers to it."

"Right." Things were becoming somewhat translucent, although my disorientation still remained. I felt at the egg-sized lump on my forehead. "A flood?" I vaguely recalled the debris and wreckage pounding against my driver's side door.

"The paperwork in your vehicle indicated that your name was Dee—is this correct?"

"Yes, it is." The stress of the moment caused my head to nod like a Betty Boop bobble doll on the dashboard of a taxi. I pointed my finger at her confidently, "My name is Dee." My memory was returning—thankfully. "Wait a minute, you said the paperwork in my vehicle? Did I lose my purse? Is my luggage gone?"

Sally shrugged. "I think so. Earl and Margie said it appeared a tree had been struck by lightning. It smashed into the trunk of your car and floodwater was gushing through your car when they pulled ya out. Sorry, that's all I know."

"I loved those sling back shoes," I whined, "and now they are gone forever."

"It could be much worse," Sally reminded me, as she energetically chewed on her mouthful of gum.

Suddenly the sight of the woman being carried away in her car rumbling along the surface of the water flashed through my mind. "There was a woman in the flood. She was in a car and I tried to call for help but I couldn't find my cellphone. Do you know if she survived?"

"I have no idea. They have been covering the flooding in West Virginia on the TV... do ya want me to turn it back on?"

"Yes, please. For just a few minutes."

The National Weather Service called the unrelenting heavy rains a "one-in-a-thousand-year event" as the Kanawha, Elk and Greenbrier Rivers crested across the state.

The bodies of three more victims of West Virginia's historic flooding were found overnight, according to county authorities, raising the death toll to twenty-six from torrential rains and high water that has destroyed more than one hundred homes, washed out scores of roads and bridges and knocked out power to tens of thousands of people.

President Obama declared a major disaster for West Virginia and ordered federal aid to supplement state and local recovery efforts in the counties of Greenbrier, Kanawha and Nicholas.

Eight to ten inches of rain fell in six to eight hours in parts of West Virginia, according to the National Weather Service.

Governor Earl Ray Tomblin told reporters that damage is wide-spread and devastating. Saying search and rescue missions are still a top priority, Tomblin issued a state of emergency for forty-four counties and deployed one hundred fifty members of the National Guard to help emergency responders. He called the flooding among the worst in a century for many parts of West Virginia.

Greenbrier Resort owner, Jim Justice, says the historic Greenbrier Resort will be closed down indefinitely because of severe damage caused by flooding. "Everything is damaged," Justice says. "We have water in the tennis building, in our chapel and our spa. It's everywhere." Justice says the last few paying guests departed on Saturday and the resort is providing food and shelter to displaced residents of the town and is raising money to benefit them. He also stated he will continue to pay employees.

The PGA Tour makes the wise decision to cancel its tournament in West Virginia as the state and the Greenbrier area recover from floods. Flooding has caused at least twenty-six deaths this week in West Virginia. A golf course and golf tournament obviously does not matter as the region tries to recover from the devastating floods, held at the Greenbrier Resort near White Sulphur Springs, an area that has been overrun by the torrential rains.

"Please, turn it off."

Sally, once again, clicked the button. "It's sad isn't it?"

"Very sad." I admitted. "Sally, how long have I been here?"

She tilted her and clasped her hands. "I'm not sure. I've been helping the doctor with some of the flood-related injuries and she asked me to come up here and sit with ya this morning. She said ya should be waking up soon."

"Who asked you?"

"Ms. Jinx, of course. She's been sitting by your side for at least three days."

"Jinx? But we were talking out in the Springhouse and she gave me a drink of the spring water." I flashed back to the story Jinx had told me about the soldier named Thomas.

"My mama sometimes brews her specialty tea using the water from the Springhouse. Usually if someone needs to cleanse their body." Jinx inserted a suction tube into the cup of tea and withdrew a fraction of the liquid. "It also works for folks who have bumped their head." She parted his lips and squirted a minuscule drop onto his tongue. "Bottoms up."

"We ate chocolate chip cookies together." I attempted to explain to Sally.

"Hey, Thomas. It's me. Jinx. I'm visiting with ya again today and decided to bring you some treats." She unwrapped a chocolate chip cookie and held it close to his nose. "Just smell this. Isn't it wonderful? I believe chocolate chip cookies smell better than anything else I can think of, don't you?" She pinched off a diminutive sliver of chocolate and placed the tiny morsel on his tongue. "If ya wake up I promise to bring ya a whole plate of cookies fresh out of the oven."

"I have no idea if you and Ms. Jinx had cookies or drank water from the Springhouse. All I know is what I've been told."
"This is all very odd."

"Thomas later told me he could hear me talking while he was sleeping, and thought I could hear him respond. He dreamed he had gone to heaven, until he opened his eyes and saw my crooked-toothed smile."

"Yep." Sally spit out her Nicorette gum into a tissue before placing three more pieces in her mouth. "It's been a very stressful few days," she told me, seemingly justifying her overuse of the product.
"Where is Jinx?"
"She said she needed to check on some family members since the water levels have subsided." She walked over to the desk sitting beneath a window,

picked up a burgundy book, and a plastic bag stuffed full of chocolate chip cookies. "Ms. Jinx said to give these to ya, and to let ya know she'll be in touch."

I pinched a tidbit of chocolate chip cookie from the bag and placed the sliver on my tongue, then delicately ran my hand over the embossed leather before disengaging the golden clasp. A faded photograph of a little girl wearing a bow in her hair fell onto my lap. *This must be a photo of Jinx.* As I turned each page I fully realized I was holding a Who's Who in the history of the United States of America, or at the very least a Who's Who in the history of the luxurious Greenbrier Hotel. *Words of wisdom imparted from Eleanor Roosevelt, Sammy Snead, Clare Boothe Luce, General Dwight D. Eisenhower, Wallis Simpson, Dorothy Draper and Bing Crosby are transcribed on these pages. Signatures from Bob Hope, John F. Kennedy, Richard Nixon, Lyndon Johnson, Paul Harvey, Billy Graham, Debbie Reynolds, Eddie Fisher, and Robert Young are sporadically scribbled inside. Judy Garland, Meyer Davis, Rose Kennedy, William Morrow, and both of Grace Kelly's parents added their autographs. Oh, there's Jinx Falkenberg and her husband, Tex McCrary. Prince Rainier and Princess Grace? Wow!*

I continued to flip through the pages and when I reached the final dedication I was stunned speechless.

To Dee,
This treasure of memories belongs to you now.
Thank you for listening to my tales,
I hope you find some of them worthy of recording.
Warmest Regards,
Jinx
June 2016

"I'll go fetch the doctor," I could hear Sally say as the door gracefully snapped shut behind her.

Present Day

So when I arrived safely at home I began investigating these stories to prove to myself that this wasn't simply a hallucination or dream. I was able to verify dates and other facts about Jinx's famous friends and fabulous tales, even down to the details of the Bethlehem mining disaster and the story concerning the ghost of Greenbrier County.

As of the day that this manuscript was sent to the publisher I was still waiting for Jinx to get in touch with me. I've even left numerous messages at the Greenbrier Hotel hoping someone would see her on the grounds and relay my eager endeavors to reach out to her. I also contacted our mutual friend, Geneva, and informed her of my urgent need to speak with Jinx.

Having in my possession one of the most elaborate collections of historical autographs I have ever seen, I know the tales I heard about during the devastating floods in West Virginia in June of 2016 were not merely my imagination; nor was it simply a fantasy brought about by a bump on the head.

So Jinx, if you are out there—I hope you approve. Thank you for sharing your stories and for steadfastly sitting beside my bed while I was recovering. I offer my unwavering gratitude for bestowing your cherished and remarkable commemorations to me.

I struggled to find the perfect quote to best portray Jinx and her mischievous personality and finally settled on a passage, which coincidentally has been misattributed to the great Eleanor Roosevelt.

According to research, Harvard Professor, Laurel Thatcher Ulrich actually coined the term in 1976. Could Eleanor have cited this phrase previously? I would not even presume to speculate. Nonetheless, I feel the following idiom adequately expresses my impression of Jinx's tales and her misadventures:

"Well behaved women seldom make history."
— *Laurel Thatcher Ulrich*

Author's Notes and Reading List

Some interesting works related to the stories contained within these pages include *Eleanor Roosevelt's Life of Soul Searching and Self Discovery*, where I discovered Eleanor was in a convent at a young age and was asked to leave because she fibbed and reported she had swallowed a coin. This book also verifies that Eleanor's mother-in-law, who lived next-door, often made comments in regards to Eleanor's appearance.

Eleanor was staying at the Greenbrier in June of 1936 as the guest speaker for the Chi Omega sorority luncheon. Additionally, according to *The Autobiography of Eleanor Roosevelt*, her insecurities during her early years eventually lessened, but it would be at least twenty-five years before Eleanor learned to "boldly walk in or walk out of any door she wants."

The Autobiography of Eleanor Roosevelt
Eleanor Roosevelt
Harper Perennial
Reprint Edition
2014

Eleanor Roosevelt's Life of Soul Searching and Self Discovery
Ann Atkins
Flash History Press LLC, Paoli, PA
2011

The book entitled *Price of Fame: The Honorable Clare Boothe Luce*, explains in great detail about her service to our country and the difficulties she faced being a woman in Congress during this particular time in United States history. Other interesting facts presented in this piece of literature are that she was, eventually, invited to dine with President and Eleanor Roosevelt, and that her first draft of the play, *The Women*, was written during a three-day stay at the Greenbrier in June of 1936.

Price of Fame: The Honorable Clare Boothe Luce
Sylvia Jukes Morris
Random House, New York
2014

Carleton Varney's, *The Draper Touch: The High Life and High Style of Dorothy Draper,* is a fabulous book, which portrays Mrs. Dorothy Draper's life and details relating to her interior designing techniques, eccentric personality, and virtuoso. The facts I found most interesting, and that confirmed the tales contained within *Jinx at the Greenbrier,* included the night Dorothy thought she saw Robert E. Lee mounted on his horse at the foot of her bed, her outrage over the wrong soap scent in the duchess' bathroom, the mix-up with hotel accommodations at the grand reopening of the Greenbrier, and that she was "fit to be tied" when *Life* magazine showcased the Duke and Duchess of Windsor on the cover instead of her.

The Draper Touch: The High Life and High Style of Dorothy Draper
Carleton Varney
Shannongrove Press, New York
1988

In *The Education of a Golfer,* by Sam Snead, the circumstances and date surrounding his arrival at the Greenbrier Hotel were confirmed. The unfortunate tale of smacking one of the C&O Board of Directors on his bootie with a long drive was also established. Additionally, he did purchase the Ashwood Methodist Church a new electric pipe organ, married Audrey, and served in the United States Navy.

The Education of a Golfer
Sam Snead
Kerygma Sellers
E-Book Edition - New edition updated by Scott Carter
2009

There is *The History of the Greenbrier: America's Resort,* written by Greenbrier's historian, Robert S. Conte, which verifies the numerous guests mentioned in this story, along with the dates they visited the hotel. There are abundant historical photographs and facts presented chronologically in *The History of the Greenbrier: America's Resort.* In addition to describing the early days of the acclaimed Greenbrier Hotel, Conte's illustrated book shows photographs of the Greenbrier when it served as Ashford General Hospital, colorful snapshots of Draper's restoration project, and details describing the Cameo Ballroom. This book is a glorious, well-written documentation of the Greenbrier Resort and its rich and noteworthy history.

The History of the Greenbrier: America's Resort
Robert S. Conte
The Greenbrier
1998

That Woman: The Life of Wallis Simpson, Duchess of Windsor is a fascinating work, which describes Wallis' early life, her relationship with King Edward VIII and their "scandal." Notations referencing the announcement by King George VI that he would create his brother the title of Duke of Windsor, and of course, the many times the couple visited the Greenbrier Hotel were also confirmed. Additionally, Wallis Simpson, the Duchess of Windsor, was very good friends with Tex and Jinx Falkenberg, as delineated within this tale.

That Woman: The Life of Wallis Simpson, Duchess of Windsor
Anne Sebba

St. Martin's Press, New York
Reprint Edition
2012

I discovered that on May 12, 1935 the Bethlehem mine in Barracksville, West Virginia did have a fire. It shot flames five hundred feet into the air. Five men were burned to death by steam and six others were injured.

http://www3.gendisasters.com/west-virginia/15291/barracksville-wv-coal-mine-fire-may-1935

The ghost story Jinx told Dorothy Draper concerning Zona, the ghost of Greenbrier County, is recorded in history. It is the only known case in which testimony from a ghost helped to convict a murderer.

http://www.wvpentours.com/greenbrier_ghost.htm

In June of 1936, Eleanor Roosevelt, Sam Snead and Clare Boothe Luce were, indeed, staying at the Greenbrier Hotel. The extensive guest list over the years included politicians, royalty, athletes, military leaders, writers, performers and many others. Greenbrier historian Robert Conte, the author of *The History of the Greenbrier: America's Resort*, developed the following exhibit of notable visitors: http://www.wvencyclopedia.org/print/ExhibitHall/19

Photo Credits

Cover photograph of the Greenbrier in 1916
https://commons.wikimedia.org/wiki/File%3AGreenbrier_Hotel_1916_
cph.3b19148.jpg

Photo of Jinx by iuliia29photo at Deposit Photos

Anna Eleanor Roosevelt, head-and-shoulders portrait,
facing slightly right.
This work is in the public domain because it was published in the
United States between 1923 and 1963 and although there may or may
not have been a copyright notice, the copyright was not renewed.
https://commons.wikimedia.org/wiki/File%3AEleanor_Roosevelt_
portrait_1933.jpg

Publicity photo of golfer Sam Snead for his ABC television program
The Sam Snead Golf Show.
This work is in the public domain because it was published in the
United States between 1923 and 1977 and without a copyright notice.
https://commons.wikimedia.org/wiki/File%3ASam_Snead_1967.JPG

Congresswoman Clare Boothe Luce of Connecticut
This United States Congress image is in the public domain.
https://commons.wikimedia.org/wiki/File%3AClare_Boothe_Luce_
(R%E2%80%93CT).jpg

The Tea Master's Blends

TEA BREWED WITH Saint John's Wort helps to soothe your worries and supports peaceful sleep.

Green tea with Ginseng is used to inspire creativity, treat forms of diabetes, as a stimulant, an aphrodisiac, and for male dysfunction.

Tea infused with Holy Basil is used to combat stress. Also known as Tulsi tea, the popular herbal brew originated in India thousands of years ago and is recognized for its rich antioxidant properties that promote wellness and longevity.

Dream Tea is a blend of Peppermint leaf, Chamomile flower, Gotu Kola, Mugwort, Rose petals, Sage and Rosemary and evokes powerful and colorful dreams that are easily recalled.

Ginger tea is used to reduce menstrual cramps, alleviate stomach pain, helps the body absorb nutrients, and can help with weight loss and to fight cancer.

Oolong tea boosts metabolism, suppresses sugar cravings and burns fat.

Royal jelly is a thick, milky substance that is fed to the queen bee in a bee colony. Some experts believe Royal jelly may improve stamina and energy. Jinx's mama added it to tea when people needed a boost of confidence.

If you have a jittery moment, a cup of Chamomile tea might help calm you down. Some compounds in Chamomile bind to the same brain receptors and prescription medications as Valium.

I sincerely hope you enjoyed *Jinx at the Greenbrier*. I would greatly appreciate your feedback with an honest review on Amazon.com.

First and foremost, I'm always looking to grow and further develop as a writer. It is reassuring to hear what works, as well as to receive constructive feedback on what should be improved. Secondly, proceeds earned from this book are donated to the Monroe County Humane Society, and the animals can always use your help.

Best regards,
Deanna Edens

Made in the USA
Middletown, DE
18 March 2021